INDUSTRY-WIDE
COLLECTIVE BARGAINING
PROMISE OR MENACE?

Problems in American Civilization
UNDER THE EDITORIAL DIRECTION OF
George Rogers Taylor

Industry-wide
Collective Bargaining

PROMISE OR MENACE?

EDITED WITH AN INTRODUCTION BY
Colston E. Warne

Problems in American Civilization

READINGS SELECTED BY THE
DEPARTMENT OF AMERICAN STUDIES
AMHERST COLLEGE

D. C. HEATH AND COMPANY: Boston

INTRODUCTION

UNDER the favorable climate of the New Deal the trade union movement flourished in the United States. Not only did old established craft unions increase in membership and in economic strength; industrial unions also emerged as a power in leading basic industries. Labor became an economic and political force to be reckoned with.

This unprecedented expansion took place during a period when both the Congress and the courts took a more friendly attitude toward labor. In the closing year of the Hoover Administration the Norris-LaGuardia Act of 1932 was passed, narrowing the scope of federal labor injunctions. The National Industrial Recovery Act of 1933 and the National Labor Relations Act of 1935 gave legislative assistance to the development of collective bargaining relationships. A sequence of court decisions broadened the exemption of unions from anti-trust laws and penalized employer interference with union growth. New and aggressive leadership arose in labor's ranks, championing industrial unionism.

As labor grew in power and prestige, national unions became increasingly interested in developing an ever-broader pattern of collective bargaining. To some observers, this pattern represented the growth of a new phenomenon in American life — that of giant labor monopoly. To others, the rise of vigorous national unions was held a natural concomitant to the integration of industrial enterprise.

It represented merely an effort to parallel an already established trend in business enterprise. Strong, responsible, and highly centralized unions were deemed essential to bring economic stability and full employment.

The current argument concerns the merits and demerits of industry-wide collective bargaining. Technically speaking, this phrase refers to the negotiation of a single agreement covering the conditions of labor in substantially an entire industry. Actually, the issue at stake between the contestants might better be characterized under the phrase "multiemployer bargaining," since the American economy is so extensive that relatively few labor agreements blanket an entire industry. The question is whether trade unionism negotiations should be confined to a local or company level or whether agreements should be reached which include, on a more or less uniform basis, a group of employers.

The problem of industry-wide bargaining first came to national attention after World War II, when many wage negotiations between employers and unionists became deadlocked. In a number of leading industries — coal, steel, railways, communications, shipping, motors, and electrical equipment — a considerable period of industrial strife ensued. While many of these industries conducted negotiations on a company-by-company basis, the feeling grew that labor had gained excessive power which should be curbed by legislative enactments. The Congressional election in 1946 gave momentum to this movement. The House of Representatives then elected was disposed to include prohibitions against industry-wide bargaining in the Taft-Hartley Bill. Indeed, Representative Fred A. Hartley, Jr. only abandoned this effort because he felt that the measure, thus amended, could not secure in Congress the votes necessary to override an expected presidential veto.

The political complexion of the 81st Congress was drastically altered as a result of the unexpected re-election of President Truman, accompanied by the retirement, temporarily at least, of many of those who earlier had championed sweeping curbs on the power of organized labor. The legislative struggle, therefore, shifted from the imposition of new prohibitions to the question of the retention of existing Taft-Hartley restraints upon trade unions.

Industry-wide bargaining remains a vital problem. In the fall of 1949, production of steel and coal was halted for more than a month when employers and unionists could not agree on the terms of new contracts. In the winter of 1950 John L. Lewis again halted coal production while he negotiated for new contracts. If persistent strikes of this type continue to paralyze our basic industries, a renewed controversy will undoubtedly emerge between those who would outlaw industry-wide bargaining and those who would accept the practice and seek other solutions to large-scale industrial disputes. Moreover, whenever a more conservative Congress is elected, the issue will undoubtedly be raised with renewed vigor.

From the readings, it will be observed that trade union leaders, though by no means unanimous, are far more unified in their approval of freedom to bargain on an industry-wide basis than employers are in their opposition. Not a few employer groups have had long and satisfactory experience with this type of bargaining and would bitterly resent its abolition by legislative enactment. Other employers, however, are not only opposed to industry-wide bargaining but also look with scant sympathy upon all types of collective bargaining. Between these two extremes are the employers who accept trade unionism but who wish to bargain on a company-by-company basis.

The proposals for constructive alternatives to industry-wide bargaining are equally numerous and conflicting. The central issue raised by not a few of these readings is whether a strong trade union movement is compatible with the successful operation of a competitive system. This broader aspect of the topic has highly significant ramifications both in the economic and political sphere. To list only a few of these — Does industry-wide bargaining advance or impair the productivity of American industry? Does industry-wide bargaining raise wages to an excessive level, based upon monopoly power, or does it contribute to a more equitable distribution of income? Does industry-wide bargaining foster democracy in an industry or does it unjustifiably limit the power of the individual employer? Does the growth of strong national unions afford a greater equalization of political power or does it represent the entrenchment of a limited group that will promote legislation suitable only to its own interests?

The first group of readings brings the issue briefly and sharply into focus by presenting the conflicting statements of former Congressman Fred A. Hartley, Jr. and the Minority Report of the Senate

Committee of Labor and Public Welfare of the 80th Congress, headed by Senator Elbert D. Thomas.

This preliminary debate is followed by a survey of the current status of collective bargaining practices, prepared by the United States Bureau of Labor Statistics. Perhaps the greatest contribution of this survey is the demonstration of the great diversity of bargaining relationships in the United States.

The third group of readings begins with an article by Professor Leo Wolman of Columbia University in opposition to industry-wide bargaining. Wolman treats the problem as one of encroaching labor monopoly which has flourished under existing legislation and court decisions. Professor Richard A. Lester, Research Associate of the Industrial Relations Section of the Department of Economics and Social Institutions of Princeton University, contends that an unrealistic and erroneous conclusion has been drawn by using the term "labor monopoly" in a manner that is applicable to commodity markets. He recognizes that many problems have been created by the widespread growth of national unions but stands in firm opposition to the bills introduced in the 80th Congress by Representative Hartley and Senator Ball. Such legislation would, he feels, "foster union rivalry, instability in labor relations, and irresponsibility in organized labor."

The economists' discussion is continued with the testimony of Professor John V. Van Sickle of Wabash College before the Senate Committee on Banking and Currency and with an excerpt from the address by Professor Edwin E. Witte of the University of Wisconsin before the 1948 Conference on Industry-wide Bargaining at the University of Pennsylvania. Van Sickle lists specific reasons

for abolishing industry-wide bargaining. Witte seeks to demonstrate the pitfalls which would follow its abolition.

The fourth group of readings includes representative statements by industrial and union leaders. Walter B. Weisenburger, Executive Vice President of the National Association of Manufacturers, expresses his faith in competitive enterprise and in collective bargaining relations between the individual company and its workers. Charles S. Craigmile of the Illinois Manufacturers' Association takes a more uncompromising position, which includes opposition not only to industry-wide bargaining but to the Wagner Act itself.

Since the bargaining relationships in bituminous coal have been particularly subject to Congressional attention due to recurrent strikes, the testimony of Tyre Taylor representing Southern coal and industrial interests is included. Taylor voices the need for legal curbs on the power of strong unions such as the United Mine Workers.

On the labor side, William Green of the American Federation of Labor, Philip Murray of the CIO, Walter Reuther of the United Automobile Workers, and John L. Lewis of the United Mine Workers oppose legislation limiting industry-wide bargaining. Green's testimony stresses the long and successful industry-wide collective bargaining relationships of the affiliates of his organization. Reuther and Murray, as CIO leaders, emphasize the growth of industrial concentration and contend that barriers should not be placed in the way of strengthening the offsetting force of organized labor.

In the testimony of John L. Lewis, a sampling is given of Lewis's views concerning the functioning of our economic system and the rights of labor under that system. He affirms that the miners' union has improved living standards only by unified action in the face of bitter opposition. The drive against industry-wide bargaining is viewed by him as an effort of organized manufacturers to undermine the labor movement.

The fifth group of readings is generally concerned with experiences under industry-wide bargaining. This section commences with excerpts from a study of the bituminous coal industry by Waldo Fisher of the Wharton School. The preface to this study, prepared by Professor George W. Taylor of the University of Pennsylvania, is inserted since it succinctly states the difficulties encountered when the mining industry resorted to individual bargaining. Fisher's conclusion, while leaning toward industry-wide bargaining, is scarcely a strong endorsement. Richard A. Lester and Edward A. Robie survey the extensive experience of seven industries with national and regional collective bargaining. This study affords strong evidence for the affirmative case as does the statement of Almon E. Roth, President of the National Federation of American Shipping, concerning the shipping industry. Opposition to industry-wide bargaining is vigorously expressed by Charles E. Wilson, President of General Motors, C. Dickerman Williams, Vice President of American Locomotive Company, and Hugh H. C. Weed, President of Carter Carburetor Corporation.

The final selection was prepared by the Twentieth Century Fund, a research organization which canvassed the views of labor and management concerning the appropriate bargaining unit. This selection, by measuring the diversity in attitudes both in the ranks of labor and in management, appears a suitable conclusion to the readings.

The problem, dealing as it does with the conflicting aspirations of thousands of companies and millions of organized workers, is indeed one for which a satisfactory solution is urgently needed. The central issue is whether the nation should lend encouragement to the growth of industry-wide bargaining, whether the nation should seek to occupy a neutral role and allow bargaining relationships to work themselves out without governmental intervention, or whether the nation should limit the unit or area of collective bargaining.

[NOTE: The statement by John V. Van Sickle on p. xii is quoted from *Industry-wide Collective Bargaining and the Public Interest* (New York, 1947), p. 5, by permission of American Enterprise Association.]

CONTENTS

The Clash of Issues

"The general adoption of industry bargaining makes for monopoly capitalism which can be nothing but a way-station on the road to socialism."

— John V. Van Sickle

"The labor monopolies of today were born in violence, short-sighted legislation, and in improper administration of the law. To deal with them effectively obviously involves extensive revision in public policy and in the administration of our labor law."

— Leo Wolman

"Statutory limitation of labor agreements to a single locality is a direct attack upon the process of free collective bargaining. Any such attempt to confine collective bargaining to a specific area will turn back the clock of industrial progress."

— William Green

"Under national or regional bargaining, wage decisions are likely to be more sensible and far-sighted, taking into consideration the economic interests of the industry as a whole, than is the case where the wage pattern for the industry is established by a wage 'leader' or by local bargaining, with the union playing one firm against another."

— Richard A. Lester and Edward A. Robie

Representative Fred A. Hartley, Jr.:

CONGRESS SHOULD OUTLAW
INDUSTRY–WIDE BARGAINING

... **I**NDUSTRY-WIDE bargaining has long been the source of many undesirable conditions within both industry and labor.

The left-wing elements in the Congress have been most outspoken against what they term a "concentration of economic power" within industry. There is no similar outcry against an equal concentration of economic power when it is lodged in labor organizations.

I am equally opposed to both.

Whenever either labor or management places too much power and authority in the hands of too small groups of men, such groups tend to reduce every worker to the lowest common denominator and every business problem to the average. As a result, agreements arrived at between such groups solve no specific problems and tend to satisfy no one since they are designed to meet average problems and average desires. Grievances arising from local conditions are a source of constant trouble, and tend to create contempt for the collective bargaining contract in many of the plants and shops covered by the master agreements.

Furthermore, and most important, industry-wide bargaining between economic giants seldom, if ever, considers the public interest.

In many industries labor costs are the largest factor in arriving at sale prices for products. Industry-wide bargaining on wages thereby removes differing wage costs from the area of competition and, in effect, stifles competition in that industry.

Wherever competition is stifled, the public suffers in the form of higher prices and inferior products.

I am well aware that one of organized labor's principal objectives is to remove wages from the area of competition, and their congressional spokesmen make a good case for this objective.

In one sense, it appears to be the contention of labor that competition on wages is but another example of the cold-blooded corporation approach to driving down the American standard of living.

This argument ignores the fact that this country is still based on a competitive economy. Admittedly, advocates of a controlled economy made great strides during the war in restricting management's freedom of action. Our experience to date indicates that it is far easier to impose such controls than to get rid of them.

Nevertheless, our economy is still a reasonably competitive one.

Competitive enterprise is one of the strongest forces in the world. Industry operated under a system of competitive free enterprise has achieved for American citizens the highest standards of

From *Our New National Labor Policy* by Fred A. Hartley, Jr. Funk and Wagnalls Company, 1948. Reprinted by permission.

living, the highest wage rates, and the shortest hours of labor of any nation.

If you love your country, you must embrace the historic competitive principle which has made our country great. If you say competition is ruthless and cold-blooded, you are, in effect, saying that America is ruthless and cold-blooded.

I don't believe that.

The first principle of statesmanship today for all of us should be to fight against any action by any economic group which tends to weaken the competitive forces which operate in our economy in any significant way. This is fundamental and goes far beyond considerations of labor law. I hope the Congress will be ever alert in recognizing this principle of statesmanship.

The original Hartley bill banned industry-wide bargaining in a comparatively simple fashion.

To begin with we limited the power of the National Labor Relations Board to certify the same individual as a representative of employees of competing employers. This prevents situations where the single head of a national union is designated as the sole bargaining agent to represent that union in its dealings with many individual employers.

To prevent injustice to small union locals situated closely together who might want to use a single representative in the interests of economy, we made an exception.

Under my bill, the NLRB could have certified a common representative for two or more union locals whenever such locals represented bargaining units of less than 100 employees and were situated within 50 miles of one another.

This limitation, you will note, placed the operation of an industry-wide system of bargaining on a voluntary basis.

Whenever a union felt it was sufficiently powerful to proceed with its collective bargaining negotiations without recourse to the processes of the NLRB, it could then designate its own bargaining representative to deal with the employers on an industry-wide basis.

The employers, on the other hand, would be under no legal compulsion to bargain with such a representative, since he would not be certified by the government as a representative of the employees for the purposes of the rewritten National Labor Relations Act.

To forestall the inevitable criticism that such a legal provision would hamstring unions in their dealings with their international offices and other affiliated organizations, we provided that no restriction would be placed on such relationships unless the collective bargaining arrangements or other concerted activities between these groups were thereby subjected to common control and approval.

This formula was not a popular one, with either management or labor. Too many industries had become accustomed to industry-wide or area-wide bargaining to want to go back to collective bargaining at the plant level. Too many big jobs in both industrial and labor circles are dependent on a continuation of this practice.

I am frank to admit that I am not completely satisfied with this formula. It was a problem where we felt it would be better to make a start this way and see how it worked in practice. Those of us who sponsored the Taft-Hartley Act in both houses of Congress were determined not to fall into the way of thought that would hold the amended National Labor Relations Act as something sacred and all-sufficient and therefore not to be amended. On the contrary if our formula for restricting industry-wide bargaining had worked to the disadvantage of the public, we would have been quick to amend the law.

During the debate on the House floor, another provision was added strengthening our restrictions on industry-wide bargaining.

This provision was proposed by Representative Kersten, a member of the labor committee. The provision made it an unlawful concerted activity for a group of employers to fix or agree to terms of employment through common control or approval whenever the employees were denied a comparable privilege.

This proposal wiped out any chance of industry-wide bargaining on any basis. While unions could have bargained industry-wide, provided they were willing to lose the benefits of NLRB support, employers would have been subject to antitrust prosecutions for similar action.

Of more significance than the restrictions placed on industry-wide bargaining were the provisions making an industry-wide strike unlawful.

While such legislation will not get at the root of many of the evils inherent in industry-wide bargaining as such, a complete ban against industry-wide strikes will weaken the economic power of a labor leader, even if he were in a position to negotiate as a representative of all the employees in an entire industry.

Furthermore, as we designed the original Hartley bill, the prohibitions against industry-wide strikes would apply to all labor organizations and their agents, regardless of their standing before the National Labor Relations Board. Consequently, those labor bosses who chose to ignore the NLRB would still have been covered by the prohibition.

In the original Hartley bill we defined an industry-wide strike as a "monopolistic" strike, as any "concerted interference with an employer's operation which results from any conspiracy, collusion, or concerted plan of acting between employees of competing employers or between representatives of such employees."

A "monopolistic" strike was further defined as an unlawful concerted activity. Unlawful concerted activities, in turn, were subjected to the Sherman Anti-Trust Act, by means of two amendments to the Clayton Act. Through another amendment, Norris-LaGuardia Act restrictions on injunctions were made inoperative in regard to such prosecutions.

The public has already suffered as a result of the omission of these particular provisions. I am convinced that such legislation, had it been enacted last year, would have saved the American people untold suffering and the loss of millions in production.

The coal strike in early spring [of 1948], for example, would have been impossible, unless John L. Lewis had been willing to expose himself to criminal prosecution under this law.

During the 80th Congress I again made an effort to get these monopolistic strike provisions enacted into law. I was not successful. But such legislation is inevitable, so long as the leaders of organized labor persist in industry-wide strikes, particularly strikes paralyzing national industry and threatening the welfare of our country. . . .

Senator Elbert D. Thomas:

CONGRESS SHOULD NOT OUTLAW INDUSTRY–WIDE BARGAINING

PROVISIONS specifically prohibiting area-wide and industry-wide collective bargaining were rejected by the [Senate] committee for inclusion in the bill as reported. We approve this action by the committee but, in view of announcements by some members of the committee that they intend to reinsert such provisions through amendments offered on the floor of the Senate, we have set forth below the considerations which motivated us in supporting the striking of such provisions from the bill.

The Bureau of Labor Statistics estimates that more than 4,000,000 workers in American industry are covered by contracts between a union and more than one employer. Some of these are industry-wide; most are regional or city-wide in character. A ban on such bargaining would disrupt existing relationships in these industries and make it necessary to renegotiate contracts covering 4,000,000 workers. Instead of negotiations resulting in a relative handful of agreements which cover thousands of employers as a group, the result would be piecemeal negotiations with thousands of individual employers, over a prolonged period of time, with thousands of individual agreements splintering the uniform standards previously achieved through industry bargaining.

Industry-wide bargaining is a logical development of present-day industrial organization. Employers are organized on an industry-wide scale; first in nation-wide corporations, and second in trade associations. Competition is nation-wide in character.

We should like to indicate what would be the effect of a ban on industry-wide bargaining on present-day industrial relations.

Any attempt to ban actions by employers to form voluntary associations for the purpose of collective bargaining would deny this group the protection accorded employee organizations. In many trades and industries, employers have joined together to bargain with unions representing their employees. In such industries as longshoring and building construction — where workers change employers from day to day or week to week — bargaining through employers' associations is the only practical method for establishing uniform wages and working conditions and eliminating cutthroat competition. . . .

Many employers prefer industry-wide or association bargaining. Mr. Vincent P. Ahearn, executive secretary of the National Sand and Gravel Association, testified before the Committee:

Some employers believe that if they could not bargain on an industry-wide basis, unions could simply isolate one employer after

From Minority Views, Federal Labor Relations Act of 1947, Committee on Labor and Public Welfare, United States Senate, 80th Congress, 1st Session, Report 105, part 2, April 22, 1947, pp. 6–7.

another and force capitulation to their demands.

This would create a situation where the weakest member of an industry would set the standard for the others.

Because numerous employers are covered by a single collective-bargaining agreement, less time is lost in the bargaining process. Settlements are made simultaneously for these employees rather than on an individual employer-by-employer basis. Industrial peace is achieved in one step, rather than over a prolonged period of time. Bargaining with hundreds of individual firms for the same things is both wasteful and unfair to both sides.

Many small employers lack the skill in bargaining and research facilities available to unions. A ban on associations of employers combining for the purpose of pooling their knowledge and resources in collective-bargaining negotiations would impair the bargaining power of employers.

Industry-wide agreement on wages protects wage standards from being undercut by lower-wage areas and lower-wage employers. By the same token, industry-wide bargaining may save individual employers from being singled out as wage leaders in their respective industries. A ban on such agreements would result in separate agreements with individual locals. Many firms control or own subsidiary plants in districts outside an immediate geographic area. Such firms would have to negotiate agreements with numerous local unions in widely scattered localities — a task that would unavoidably become snarled up in wage differentials and eventually would revive the old cutthroat competition and the law of the jungle between company and company, between area and area.

Barring joint activities of local unions and reducing the function of international unions to that of an advisory body should, in fairness, require the same treatment for corporations with plants scattered widely over the country.

The charge is made that industry-wide bargaining leads to industry-wide strikes which threaten the public welfare. We should like to emphasize that it is not the character of the bargaining which brings about major strikes, but the organized joint refusal of that industry's employers to meet the union's demands. Under company-by-company bargaining, employers would try to drive standards down to the level of the lowest in the industry, and unions would seek to attain the level of the highest, and the result would be an epidemic of strikes throughout the various units of the industry.

A ban on industry-wide bargaining would minimize the role of the international union and prohibit it from exercising its authority to intervene in strikes of its affiliates; and prevent it from employing its prestige in its own industry for moderation and restraining counsel.

In order for the Senate fully to realize the potential impact of a ban on industry-wide bargaining by large geographical areas, we call attention to a study recently prepared by the Bureau of Labor Statistics which shows the extent of bargaining in specific industries with associations and groups of employers.*. . .

* [Reproduced on page 6. Ed.]

United States Bureau of Labor Statistics:

COLLECTIVE BARGAINING WITH ASSOCIATIONS AND GROUPS OF EMPLOYERS

MOST of the examples of industry-wide bargaining in the United States are the product of generations of experience, and as a rule the employer-union relations in these industries have been remarkably stable and peaceful. In the pressed or blown glassware industry, one of the branches of glass and glassware having national bargaining, no major strike throughout the industry has occurred since collective bargaining began with an employers' association in 1888. Similar conditions have prevailed in the pottery industry since 1922. The 1946 contract between the National Automatic Sprinkler and Fire Control Association and the United Association of Journeymen Plumbers and Steamfitters (AFL) is a revision of the original agreement of 1915; and the 1946 agreement between the Anthracite Coal Operators and the United Mine Workers of America (AFL) is a compilation of resolutions, revisions, rulings, and decisions dating back to 1903. Bargaining on an industry basis exists in the elevator installation and repair, installation of automatic sprinklers, pottery and related products, stove making, and wall-paper industries, and in coal mining.

Agreements covering all the employers in an industry within a geographic region are somewhat more numerous than those having application throughout an entire industry. Even more numerous are the instances in which associations or groups of employers are dealt with on a city-wide or metropolitan area basis. . . .

Few of the examples of collective bargaining on an industry, geographic, or city basis occurred in the mass-production industries, although a single agreement in the automobile industry, for instance, may cover many more employees than an association agreement covering every employer in an industry or trade within the same city. In mass-production industries, trends are developing toward standardized conditions in large segments of industries through corporation-wide collective bargaining. The efforts of unions are directed first toward bringing all the plants of a given large corporation, regardless of geographic location, within the scope of a single agreement. An example is the corporation-wide bargaining between the Ford Motor Co. and the United Automobile, Aircraft and Agricultural Implement Workers of America (CIO). Notwithstanding the great number of workers affected, corporation-wide bargaining differs widely from multi-employer collective bargaining which is the subject of the present study.

From Bulletin No. 897 of the United States Department of Labor, Bureau of Labor Statistics.

Early in 1947, more than 4 million workers were covered by agreements negotiated between trade-unions and associations and groups of employers. These are about equally divided between manufacturing and nonmanufacturing industries. Approximately a fourth of all workers covered by union agreements in manufacturing and a third of such workers in nonmanufacturing are working under agreements negotiated with groups or associations of employers. The agreements were negotiated by one or more unions (1) with a formal or informal association of employers or (2) with informal multi-employer groups. In presenting the information on agreements, no attempt was made to distinguish between agreements with associations and with other multi-employer groups. Identical agreements signed by separate employers with the same union were included, if there appeared to have been negotiations with a group or committee of employers.

In table 1, the extent of association and employer-group bargaining is shown, based upon the percent of total workers under agreement in the respective industries. The industries are classified by area of bargaining in table 2.

TABLE 1. — *Percent of All Workers Under Agreement Who Are Covered by Agreements With Associations and Groups of Employers, by Industry*

80–100 percent	60–79 percent	40–59 percent	20–39 percent
Clothing, men's	Baking	Building service and	Beverages, non-
Clothing, women's	Book and job print-	maintenance	alcoholic
Coal mining	ing and publishing	Leather products,	Hosiery
Laundry and clean-	Canning and pre-	other	Hotels and
ing and dyeing	serving foods	Newspaper and peri-	restaurants
Longshoring	Construction	odical printing and	Jewelry and silver-
Maritime	Dyeing and finishing	publishing	ware
Shipbuilding and	textiles		Lumber
boatbuilding[1]	Glass and glassware		Shoes, cut stock and
	Malt liquors		findings
	Pottery and related		Trade
	products		
	Trucking and ware-		
	housing		

0–19 percent

Agricultural machinery and	Cement	Cotton textiles
tractors	Chemicals, excluding rayon	Confectionery products
Aircraft and parts	and allied products	Crude petroleum and natu-
Automobiles and parts	Clerical and professional,	ral gas
Bus and streetcar, local	excluding transportation,	Dairy products
Bus lines, intercity	communication, theaters,	Electrical machinery, equip-
Carpets and rugs, wool	and newspapers	ment and appliances

[1] During World War II most of the industry was covered by tripartite zone standard agreements, signed by representatives of unions, employers, and certain government agencies. The principal association agreement other than the zone standard agreements is between Pacific Coast Shipbuilders and the Metal Trades Department of the AFL, covering yards organized by AFL unions.

Flour and other grain products
Furniture
Knit goods, except hosiery
Leather (tanned, curried and finished)
Light and power
Machinery and machine tools
Meat packing
Metal mining
Motorcycles, bicycles, and parts
Newspaper offices
Nonferrous metals and products, except jewelry and silverware
Nonmetallic mining and quarrying
Paper and pulp
Paper products
Petroleum and coal products, except refining
Petroleum refining
Railroad equipment
Rayon and allied products
Rubber products
Silk and rayon textiles
Steel, basic
Steel products
Stone and clay products, other
Sugar, beet and cane
Telegraph service and maintenance
Telephone service and maintenance
Tobacco manufactures
Woolen and worsted textiles

TABLE 2. — *Area of Bargaining With Associations or Groups of Employers, by Industry*

Bargaining on a national or industry-wide scale	Bargaining by geographic (regional) areas	Bargaining within a city, county, or metropolitan area
Coal mining	Canning and preserving foods[1]	Baking
Elevator installation and repair	Dyeing and finishing textiles[1]	Beverages, nonalcoholic
Glass and glassware	Fishing	Book and job printing and publishing
Installation of automatic sprinklers	Hosiery	Building service and maintenance
Pottery and related products	Leather (tanned, curried, and finished)[1]	Clothing, men's[2]
Stoves	Longshoring[1]	Clothing, women's[2]
Wall paper	Lumber[1]	Confectionery products
	Maritime	Construction
	Metal mining	Cotton textiles
	Nonferrous metals and products, except jewelry and silverware[1]	Dairy products
	Paper and pulp	Furniture[2]
	Shoes, cut stock and findings[1]	Hotel and restaurant
		Jewelry and silverware
		Knit goods
		Laundry and cleaning and dyeing
		Leather products, other
		Malt liquors
		Meat packing
		Newspaper printing and publishing
		Paper products, except wall paper
		Silk and rayon textiles
		Steel products, except stoves[2]
		Tobacco
		Trade[2]
		Trucking and warehousing[2]

[1] There also is some bargaining on a city, county, and/or metropolitan area basis.
[2] There also is some bargaining on a regional and/or industry-wide basis.

. . . Although industry-wide trade associations have come to be a common characteristic of American business, the scope of employer groups or associations engaged in collective bargaining is generally much more limited. Within an industry, employers may be organized for purposes of collective bargaining on a city, regional or, in a few instances, nation-wide basis, or two or more such employer organizations may exist in the same area. As a rule, the unions work toward the extension of the collective-bargaining agreement to as wide a section of the industry as possible. In a number of cases the unions and employer organizations together have directed their efforts toward bringing unorganized sections of the industry within the scope of collective-bargaining agreements. A necessary corollary of dealing through employers' associations is a high degree of unionization among the employees. . . .

The attention directed to a few national associations with long records of collective bargaining should not be permitted to obscure thousands of employer organizations which have negotiated agreements on a regional or metropolitan basis and which affect hundreds of thousands of workers. These employer groups vary widely as to type, structure, procedure, and scope of activity. Some are temporary and highly informal, with no tangible evidences of permanent organization. Others have complex structures with elaborate constitutions and a staff of full-time employees. Between these extremes there are wide variations in organization, procedures, and functions.

Nation-wide Collective Bargaining in the Coal Industry

In anthracite mining a single agreement is signed to cover the entire industry. In bituminous-coal mining, the union negotiated agreements with the operators in the Central Competitive Field (Ohio, Indiana, Illinois, and West Virginia) from 1898 until 1927. The agreement for this area set the pattern for negotiations in other areas between districts of the union and local associations of coal-mine operators. The interstate bargaining relationship in the Central Competitive Field collapsed in 1927 and was not reestablished until after the passage of the National Industrial Recovery Act. In 1934 an agreement was signed with the operators in the Appalachian area which served, as the previous interstate agreement had, as a pattern which the remainder of the industry generally followed. Districts of the United Mine Workers of America negotiate agreements with parallel associations of employers, which follow the terms of the Appalachian agreement. In 1941 the northern and southern groups of operators in the Appalachian area signed separate agreements with the union, and unified negotiations were not reestablished until 1945. In that year, the first industry-wide agreement in bituminous-coal mining was negotiated. . . .

National Bargaining on the Railroads

The traditional bargaining unit in railroad transportation is the individual railroad system. The workers are organized on the basis of craft, and agreements with the various systems are negotiated by each craft union or by "system federations" of shop craft unions. Although the regular working agreements continue to be signed by systems, on occasion certain specific questions of major importance, as wages, have been settled on a nation-wide basis. Negotiations are generally conducted by the nonoperating unions (clerical, maintenance, and shop crafts) and by the operating unions (train and engine service) separately with representatives of the railroads selected on a regional basis.

Other Industry or Trade-wide Bargaining

The American examples of trade-wide bargaining of longest status occur in the pottery and glassware industries. Since the early years of this century, an annual meeting has been held between the representatives of the United States Potters' Association and the National Brotherhood of Operative Potters. The current agreement between these parties, for example, continues a provision for joint discharge committees first set up in 1913. Since 1888 the National Association of Manufacturers of Pressed and Blown Glassware, or its predecessor, has been meeting with the American Flint Glass Workers Union. The "Star Island Agreement" of 1903 established a grievance procedure which still is utilized in this industry. The Glass Bottle Blowers' Association of the United States and Canada signed its first national agreement in 1890 and currently has an agreement with the Glass Container Manufacturers' Institute which affects several thousand employees in the industry. . . .

A different kind of bargaining relationship has been built up in the manufacture of flat glass. By far the major part of the production in this industry is centralized in two large producing companies. These companies, the Pittsburgh Plate Glass Co. and the Libby-Owens-Ford Glass Co., negotiate their agreements jointly, both with the Window Glass Cutters League (AFL) and the Federation of Glass, Ceramic and Silica Sand Workers (CIO), but each company signs separate, identical agreements. The two companies also collaborate in the administration of the agreement to insure uniform patterns of interpretation. Most of the other manufacturers are organized into the Fourcault Manufacturers' Association which negotiates the agreement with the unions.

There are a few other instances of industry-wide dealing, each of them originating from the efforts of a highly skilled craft to protect its conditions of employment. . . .

Industry-wide Bargaining in Mass-production Industries

In the more recently organized, mass-production industries there are at present no examples of industry-wide collective bargaining resulting in a single union agreement covering the full range of employer-union relations. In a few such industries, however, certain bargaining relationships have come into existence which produce considerable uniformity in the agreements throughout an industry. . . .

A degree of standardization has been achieved in the meat-packing industry through the medium of uniform expiration dates of the agreements with the principal packers. Certain agreements affecting a large number of workers negotiated by the United Packinghouse Workers of America (CIO) and by the Amalgamated Meat Cutters and Butcher Workmen of North America (AFL), covering various plants of the four largest corporations in the industry, have expired on the same day each year for several years.

Negotiation of Similar Agreements in the Steel Industry

In the basic steel industry in the United States there is no employers' association which engages in collective bargaining, yet a great deal of standardization in industrial relations has occurred in recent years. The industry is composed of two dominant groups of employers, one known as "Big Steel" and the other as "Little Steel." The first includes the United States Steel Corp. and its subsidiaries, and the second is made up of a number of independent companies. The Steel Workers Organizing Committee, now the United Steelworkers of America, first signed written agreements with the U. S. Steel Corp. in 1937 and since then, with a few exceptions, practically all of the basic steel industry has been brought under agreement. Even though there is no bargaining by employers' associations, the major provisions of agreements throughout the basic steel industry are similar. This degree of uniformity is occasioned by a number of factors, first among them probably being the predominant position of the United States Steel Corp. Agreements with this corporation tend to set the pattern for the rest of the industry. Also, by long-established practice the same wage adjustments generally are made throughout the industry at the same time. During World War II directives of the National War Labor Board, which generally were applicable to large sections of the industry, further encouraged the growth of uniform collective-bargaining practices. The United Steelworkers of America, the most important union in the industry, also tended to bring a degree of uniformity into the bargaining relationships and practices. . . .

Collective Bargaining by Geographic Areas

In the hosiery industry a bargaining relationship has existed between the Full-Fashioned Hosiery Manufacturers of America, Inc., and the American Federation of Hosiery Workers since 1927. The employers' association, originally covering only Philadelphia mills, now covers a major part of the northern section of the full-fashioned hosiery industry. Conferences occur annually, with occasional additional meetings on specific subjects. Under the agreement the joint relations are administered by a permanent impartial chairman.

In the textile industry there are association agreements between the Textile Workers' Union of America and associations of silk and rayon mills in a number of States. A joint arrangement of longer standing exists in the dyeing and finishing of textiles in nonintegrated mills. In cotton textiles in Massachusetts and in knit goods in Philadelphia and New York, many of the employers are members of associations which negotiate union agreements.

Maritime workers usually deal with employer organizations which represent the shipping operators on a given coast. Practically all the union agreements in the maritime industry are negotiated with associations or informal committees representing the employers. On the Pacific Coast the companies are organized into the Pacific American Shipowners Association. On the Atlantic and Gulf Coasts the most recent agreements were negotiated and signed by a Committee for Companies and Agents, Atlantic and Gulf Coasts, most of the members of which are also members of the American Merchant Marine Institute.

The Waterfront Employers of the Pacific Coast embraces employers of longshoremen along the entire West Coast; much of the work of the association, however, is carried on through affiliated local Waterfront Employers Associations in Seattle, Portland, San Francisco, and San Pedro (Los Angeles). The International Longshoremen's and Warehousemen's Union (CIO) negotiates a general cargo agreement with the coast-wide association, which signs "on behalf of" the four local organizations. Separate agreements covering dock workers and ship clerks are negotiated with each of the port associations. On the Atlantic Coast the International Longshoremen's Association (AFL) as a rule, negotiates separate agreements with employer associations in each port.

In the Pacific Northwest the pulp and paper industry, although dealing elsewhere on the basis of individual companies, is combined into the Pacific Coast Association of Pulp and Paper Manufacturers which deals with the two national unions in the field. . . .

The lumber industry is one which is not yet well organized throughout the country but in which the dominant method of present dealing is through associations within the producing area. The Columbia Basin Loggers' Association and the Timber Producers' Association in Minnesota are examples of associations dealing with the union in this industry.

The fishing industry, particularly on the Pacific Coast where it is well organized, is an example of collective bargaining almost exclusively on an association basis. The employers, however, are organized into a number of separate associations, such as the Alaska Packers' Association and the Central Pacific Wholesale Fish Dealers' Association. . . .

Most of the shipbuilding and boatbuilding industry on the West Coast is covered by a master agreement negotiated by the Metal Trades Department of the American Federation of Labor. . . .

Bargaining in the Needle Trades Within Metropolitan Areas

Outstanding examples of stable bargaining relationships over a long period of time between employers' associations and unions are found in the needle trades. In the men's and women's clothing, men's hats and millinery, and fur industries the earliest efforts of unions to organize were accompanied by efforts to combine into associations the employers within the producing area. Bargaining has become established in these industries, with highly developed industrial relations machinery within each of the metropolitan areas which are important as producing centers. These unions and employers' associations customarily make use of a permanent impartial chairman to administer the agreement and there are numerous examples of joint trade boards, stabilization commissions, and other similar bodies which deal on a day-to-day basis with the problems of the industry.

These industries all have the problem of "run-away" shops, which leave the unionized areas and, with the small capital investment required, are able to establish themselves in low-wage, semirural sections. This has been a major reason for the unions' insistence upon dealing on an association basis, for it is through the combined pressure of both the union and the employer association that these "run-away" shops can be brought under control. Another problem within these industries is the regulation of the jobber-contractor relationship. Jobbers have taken advantage of both the extreme seasonal fluctuations and the small investment required in setting up a shop to encourage an oversupply of contractors. Cut-throat competition among the contractors has been furthered by the frequent practice of establishing "fly by night" shops for the duration of a contract secured by underbidding regularly operating shops. Both the owners of shops operating under union conditions and their workers have thus faced a constant threat to industrial stability. Through collective bargaining, the over-supply of contractors has been dealt with and the jobber's responsibility for maintaining union conditions in his contract shops has been established. A large portion of the employer-union negotiations in the needle trades deal with these three-way problems, in addition to the usual wages, hours, and working conditions.

The employers within a given city are usually organized into more than one association within each of the needle trades. The basis of distinction is both the type of product and the classification of employers (i.e., jobbers, contractors, or inside manufacturers). The unions

have frequently expressed a desire for more uniformity among the employers' organizations throughout the industry. Although a major part of the production in the country is covered by the New York City agreements alone, the unions have made repeated efforts over several decades to secure industry-wide dealing in the interests of national standardization. Thus far, however, only in men's clothing has there been a successful approach to industry-wide bargaining. For a number of years the Amalgamated Clothing Workers of America has negotiated major wage questions with the Clothing Manufacturers' Association of the United States and with the Shirt Industry.

Leo Wolman: INDUSTRY–WIDE BARGAINING

THE people of the United States have had many opportunities in recent years to see what happens when one union or a combine of unions controls the labor force of an entire industry. Each year since the end of the war the United Mine Workers has struck. Each time it has effectively cut off the coal supply of the country because the employers refused to grant the union's demands. Each time the result has been a spreading paralysis of industry and trade. In the railroad industry we have had one national strike and the threat of another. In the automobile and steel industries, not to speak of others, a wage and contract settlement with one important company has become, for all practical purposes, the settlement for all other

companies because the unions of automobile and steel workers have the power to impose their terms on all employers, whether or not they have seriously bargained over and arrived at these terms by voluntary agreement.

These are the facts. But what are their causes? How did these events come to be? And what is to be done about them? On the railroads and in coal mining, industry bargaining is a matter of formal contract. In the more recently organized automobile, steel and electrical manufacturing industries, and in a score of other industries, the same results are accomplished without a general, formal agreement. In either case, whether the terms of collective contracts are arrived at in one way or the other, this trend toward

From *Industry-wide Bargaining* by Leo Wolman. Foundation for Economic Education, Inc., 1948. Reprinted by permission.

"industry-wide bargaining" is fraught with political and economic consequences which are little understood by the public as well as by the parties to organized labor relations. These consequences affect the welfare of every man, woman and child in this and in every other country. Any effort to clarify this problem, therefore, should clearly be an educational responsibility of first-rate importance.

In its pure form, industry-wide bargaining exists when one or several unions, acting together, bargain with an employers' association over wages and working conditions for an entire industry. The contracts or agreements apply to all of the firms or employers in the industry. In practice, industry-wide bargaining in this extreme form is rare in the United States. But something close to it exists in the railroad and bituminous coal industries, where, for all practical purposes, the unions and the employers' associations usually legislate for everybody in the industry — company and employee.

More common than systems of industry-wide bargaining are regional and local systems. In these, employers in a city or wider area join together to bargain for the industry in that area or region with the union or unions representing their employees. Such "multiple-employer" bargaining may cover an entire industry or a part of it, or it may cover the employers of diverse industries in a given area. Good examples are the local arrangements in the building industry in many parts of the country and the arrangements prevailing in San Francisco between the San Francisco Employers' Council and various unions in that city.

Under arrangements of this kind, a chief purpose is to fix uniform scales of wages and uniform working conditions within an entire industry or area. Uniformity may not always be achieved; and where it is achieved, it may not last or may be interrupted. But uniformity is still the goal. There are often obstacles in the way of getting it, but the struggle to surmount them goes on.

To many laymen, and even to some professional students of labor problems, there seems to be nothing wrong with this aim or policy. It seems natural to move from bargaining with a single employer to dealing with a group of employers and then with an entire industry acting as a unit. The objectives appear valid and reasonable. Each party to the arrangement is considered to be within his rights. Essential interests are being protected. The scheme of things frequently looks like "stability," and any policy which lays claims to promoting stability is assumed to be correct and good.

This appeared, until recently, anyhow, to be the prevailing public opinion toward such devices as industry-wide and multiple-employer bargaining. The subject was never even mentioned in the halls of Congress. Only in the past few years has there been a noticeable shift in opinion. And with this shift in opinion, the whole subject of bargaining by industry has come to be regarded as the single most important issue of labor relations and public policy toward the labor problem.

It is no accident, therefore, that the first session of the Eightieth Congress should have given extended attention to this question, and that the legislative proposals for dealing with it should have become the subject of bitter debate. In the task of revising the nation's labor law, to which this session was largely devoted, the matter of the scope of collective bargaining elicited the most novel proposals for altering existing legislation, as both Senate and House bills undertook to restrict the area of bargaining. . . .

The Setting

What obviously focused public attention on the systems of union-employer relations in the United States was the unparalleled growth of unionism since 1935. From 1935 to 1940, union membership increased from 3,650,000 to 8,100,000. By 1947, there had been added another six million, bringing the total to 14,300,000. In 1948, the number was still rising.

There is no parallel to such an expansion of trade unionism in the entire history of the country. In an earlier period of union growth, during World War I, membership advanced from something over 2,500,000 in 1914 to 5,000,000 in 1920. No comparable expansion of unions, in so short a time, can be found in other industrial countries of the world, unless the peculiar and unique growth of the Russian unions since the revolution is considered comparable to what has happened to the so-called "free" labor movements of England and Western Europe. . . .

In a little more than a decade, unionism radically changed its position in the United States. From a small minority, representing most of the time little more than ten per cent of the nonagricultural wage-earning and salaried population, it rose in these last years to a minority empowered to speak for forty per cent. It is only natural that so great a shift in absolute and relative power should shortly place old and familiar questions in a new perspective. It was to be expected that a public which viewed the behavior of a small and relatively weak minority with equanimity and indifference should begin to take seriously the same practices in the hands of a larger

and much more powerful minority. If nothing else had changed, the new minority was certainly much more likely than the old to be able to enforce its demands.

This was not the only change in the position of organized labor. In the long industrial history of this country preceding the last decade, trade unionism was a limited movement. It was consistently strong in building and on the railroads; occasionally so in coal mining and clothing; firmly embedded in such crafts as those of actors, theatrical stage employees, musicians and printers. Beyond this, there was little or no organization. The extensive manufacturing industries of iron and steel, machinery, food, textiles and automobiles; mining other than coal; transportation other than railroads; public utilities; trade and commerce; the services — all were practically unorganized. Whatever labor movement there was in the United States before 1935 was segregated in a handful of industries and crafts.

With the increase in total membership, large segments of these unorganized industries were rapidly unionized. In the services, unions are still weak; and in wholesale and retail trade, though union membership is rising, it constitutes a small percentage of those employed. But the balance of industries formerly nonunion became largely union. In a decade the leading manufacturing industries were organized. So were trucking, water transportation, air transport, the electric light and gas industries and metal mining — not to speak of an extensive and heterogeneous group of employees hitherto unorganized and, until recently, unorganizable.

This transformation in the position of organized labor had swift practical consequences. Union policies and practices which previously affected only the fringes of American industry now went to its very heart. Single unions or combinations of them now had the power to shut off the flow of innumerable goods and services, or to determine the conditions under which it was allowed. In a country in which the right of men and women to strike was freely granted, this was the first time that organized labor was strong enough to shut down any one of a long list of important and often essential economic activities. With the disappearance of limited unionism, there was the threat of the disappearance of the limited strike. As the labor movement became more or less universal, the public increasingly faced the risk, in times of labor trouble, of being deprived of a variety of goods and services and of their competitive substitutes.

The rise and spread of organized labor, therefore, aroused public concern simply because what had before been restricted had now become general. Featherbedding attracted hardly any attention so long as it was practiced only in the building and railroad industries and by musicians, but it rose to the position of a major political issue when it promised to become a universal labor policy. The right to strike, in recent decades denied only by extremists, took on a wholly different complexion once exercise of the right threatened recurrent industrial paralysis and crises and endangered the people's health and safety. In a country long hostile to monopoly of any sort, the far-flung development of union monopoly could hardly be expected to pass unnoticed and, in the long run, untouched.

At the center of these changes and fears stands the national union, the highest stage in the evolution of trade union government. The national union binds diverse local and occupational unions into a central organization. As a rule, it is the custodian of the union's financial resources, the center of power and the originator of policy. Local constituencies are held in line through the discipline imposed by the union's national, or central, office. Like most popular organizations, the national union is ruled by an extensive political machine which, once it is firmly established, is necessarily concerned with perpetuating itself in office. It is only natural that an organization of this type should be moved by various, and often conflicting, considerations. It is usually not unaware of the economic course best calculated to serve the interest of its members. But as a political machine, concerned with augmenting the power of the union, it often decides to use the methods and strategy best calculated to serve the interest of the organizations, whether or not the resulting policies are sound and beneficial to the members. Whenever these interests come into conflict, as they invariably do, one must give way to the other. It is not inconceivable that there should be frequent occasions when the members' interest is subordinated to the interest of the union.

We have in the national union, therefore, a species of private political machine or government which, in the nature of the case and in common with all governments, is engaged in furthering its own special ends. In 1947, there were some two hundred such national unions in the United States, the majority of them being organizations of substantial size. The following seven national unions claimed, in 1947, between 500,000 and 1,000,000 members and exercised jurisdiction over a wide range of industry:

Union	1947 Membership
United Steel Workers (CIO)	858,000
United Automobile Workers (CIO)	836,000

Machinists' Union (Independent) . 650,000
Brotherhood of Teamsters (AFL) . 625,000
United Electrical and Radio Work-
    ers (CIO) 625,000
United Mine Workers (Independ-
    ent) 600,000
Brotherhood of Carpenters (AFL) 600,000

Aside from everything else, organizations of this type constitute large and valuable vested interests, which, once they have been acquired, the union officialdom is loath to surrender. Although national unions possess extensive powers, many of them analogous to the powers of government, they are essentially private institutions. What they do lies in large measure within their own discretion; and their authority to make laws on matters which go far beyond the immediate, and often narrow, interests of the union and its members is subject to few practical restrictions.

The extent of the area over which they claim jurisdiction and for which they make the policies governing working conditions is determined by their own arbitrary decisions. The United Steel Workers, for example, has in its short life organized an infinite variety of shops, all of which it elects to classify under the steel industry and in which it then attempts to apply, usually with marked success, common rules. The United Mine Workers, pursuing a similar imperialistic design, by a simple revision of its constitution, converted itself overnight from a union composed exclusively of coal miners to an organization of coal miners plus chemical, plastic, building, clothing and other employees. . . .

The national union, being what it is, is an instrument ideally suited for the practice of monopoly. The typical national union is constantly redefining and extending the boundaries of the competitive area for which it stakes its claim. The avowed purpose of the undertaking is to restrain, reduce or eliminate competition in anything that may be defined as a condition of work. The grand aim of a labor movement is to raise all standards of pay and working conditions, and to see to it that no one falls behind the leader of the procession. Therefore, the main objective of the national union is to remove all labor conditions from the influence of competition.

In the years since 1935, these actual and potential restraints on competition have become more formidable than they ever were before. One reason for this is that they are today, because of the expansion of trade unionism, more extensively practiced than in the past. Second, the list of issues which are subject to joint negotiation and collective bargaining is much longer than it was ten years ago, and is still being extended under the influence of public policy, decisions of the National Labor Relations Board and the effective demands of the unions. Third, unionism is spreading to industries which customarily competed one against the other — as, for example, trucking competed against the railroads, oil against coal, etc. In these days, the common run of industries is already organized, or is rapidly becoming so; and it is the accepted policy for one union to reach for the higher standards of another. The result, therefore, is to reduce competition between industries as well as within them. Competition is thus attacked from two directions — inside an industry and between industries that normally compete with each other. This tendency does not take into account the efforts of strong pressure groups, like the modern unions, to use their political influence to block the establishment of competitive enterprises.

In these recent developments in organized labor and labor relations, the federal government took a leading and decisive part. Clearly, in the absence of government intervention there would have been nothing like the spread of unionism such as that which has taken place since 1935. A succession of federal laws to promote unionism began with the Railway Labor Act of 1926 and reached its climax in the Wagner Act of 1935. These laws were supported by numerous federal administrative agencies whose functions directly or indirectly touch the labor situation. These laws and agencies not only removed existing obstacles to unionization, but deliberately promoted the expansion of labor unions. In addition, there was widespread failure of local courts and police to enforce the laws against assault and intimidation and against illegal seizure of property by union pickets. In many cases the police actually helped the pickets keep nonunion workers away from their jobs on the grounds that they were thereby helping "keep the peace." In this process of unionizing the labor force, the dividing line between lawful and unlawful practices, between sound and unsound public policy, was slight. In retrospect, it is fair to say that at no time in these years were the probable consequences of the country's labor policies carefully examined and appraised.

A decade's experience with a vastly expanded labor movement has deeply affected American opinion. Conclusions previously held are no longer taken for granted. For many participants in labor relations, and for many students of the labor situation, the rise of a universal labor movement and the way such a movement deals with the country's industry have raised novel and unforeseen problems. The question is what the most critical of these problems are. . . .

The Future of the Problem

What, then, is the labor relations pattern which has thus been established in the United States? Several hundred national unions to which more than fourteen million employees owe voluntary or compulsory allegiance appear firmly established. Among the popular organizations of these times, they are easily the most powerful. By custom and, in large measure, by law, they are answerable to no one. In view of the complexity and variety of matters with which they deal, consultation with a rank-and-file of 100,000 or 800,000 members is a pure formality. Acceptance of proposals by the members is assured by the way the proposition is put and by the skillful and effective propaganda which gets under way long before the "union's" demands are finally formulated. Often the members are required to take a position on matters of little direct interest or concern to them. This is clearly the case with many "sympathetic" strikes, which are usually inspired and directed by the union's central office. The numerous strikes in war plants and in the coal mines to force the unionization of foremen and the recognition of foremen's unions would not have been initiated by the men in factories and mines. The recent rejection by the national office of the United Automobile Workers of a liberalized plan of insurance offered by General Motors to its employees was clearly not a response to pressure from union members, since a large number of them had already accepted the plan and recognized it as much superior to what they had. The union, with its own prestige in mind, preferred no plan to one for which it received no "credit."

The theory on which the national union operates is essentially monopolistic. This is shown by the zeal and persistence with which it seeks to extend its authority over all parts of the competitive area. No union, however large and powerful, ever stops organizing. A single nonunion employer in a highly populous industry is considered a menace to the union, even if his economic advantage consists not of lower wages or longer hours but of greater freedom to manage than his organized competitors have succeeded in retaining. Once they achieve or approximate full control over a competitive industry, national unions become, next to the government, the most effective cost-and-price-raising instruments of modern times. In the long run, they have this effect, not only by reason of their wage policies, but through the ways they limit the right to manage and devise elaborate and cumulative restrictions of output.

Collective bargaining operates by rules. The older and more "successful" a system of collective bargaining is, the larger is the number of rules and the more stringent their application. It is not surprising, under the circumstances, that the range of management's discretion should be progressively narrowed. The process is an insidious and subtle one. In its early stages it is hardly noticed. But after a decade or two the effects are marked and unmistakable. The climax of this sort of development can be observed in the nationalized British coal mines, where the more resourceful and imaginative mine managers are resigning because they no longer enjoy the right to manage. No great contribution can be made to an understanding of the future problems of labor relations in the United States than a comprehensive and detailed study of what happened to management after generations of collective bargaining in England. It would be an arduous and expensive undertaking. But it would be more than worth the money. . . .

In union policy, restriction of output stands usually on the same footing with wages, hours, discipline, seniority and other conditions of work. What a union normally promises when it is campaigning for new members is less work for the same or more money. Union labor is also predisposed to restriction of output because of long indoctrination with the evils of machinery, speed-up, stretch-out and the like. What people forget about the labor situation in the United States, in contrast, say, with England, is that here prevailing work habits and efficiency were well established in most industries long before the recent rise of organization. What the future holds is another matter. The late arrival of large-scale unionism in the United States, deplored by many as one of the great evils of American industrialism, may turn out to be a blessing in disguise. Certainly the record of labor relations in the few industries which have been unionized for many years, e.g., the building trades and railways, is not such as to inspire confidence in the future of labor relations in steel, automobiles, textiles and other industries.

It is also forgotten that in the few nationally competitive industries in which unions flourished before 1935, the efficacy of union restrictions was often checked by the unorganized employees. It was this condition, in fact, that kept these unions from winning control over an entire competitive area and engaging in industry-wide bargaining or its equivalent. Since 1935 unions, with the extraordinary assistance of government, have been rapidly removing this check on union domination.

How the absence of national control and industry-wide bargaining affects the capacity of a union to practice restriction effectively is suggested in a description by exceptionally well-informed students of precisely such a situation in the full-fashioned hosiery industry. Writing of competitive producing areas, George W. Taylor and G. Allan Dash, Jr., say:[1]

The second period of rapid expansion in the demand for full-fashioned hosiery, which began in 1935 and continued through 1940, has been characterized by severe competition between the long-established mills in the north and the more recently established mills in the south. This competition was engendered to no little extent by the requirement of labor agreements that union shops must adhere to the single-machine method of operation. Although there were strong social reasons for not adopting the double-machine system of operation, which would involve hiring helpers for whom knitting jobs would never be available, the continuance of the single-machine system meant that the older equipment of the north could not be operated at the lowest possible costs. The construction of longer section and faster machines was thereby accelerated, although the non-union territories were the only ones financially able to install the new equipment, and the machinery capacity of the industry as a whole was again boosted. Although labor rates, overhead, and profits were reduced on the single-machine system, they never caught up with the costs on the more productive machines.

These developments in labor relations raise broader questions than their economic consequences. The national union is another institution devoted to the centralization of authority over wide-spread and remote constituencies. It requires for its successful administration the creation of an extensive hierarchy of officials, much after the manner of centralized

governments, which the members must support. Local decisions which are not in tune with the purposes of the national union are overruled. A decision to strike must be obeyed whatever the members may think about it. If some of them would like to go to work when a national strike is on, they are kept idle by mass picketing, with the pickets recruited from other communities, as has often happened in coal strikes and has today become a common occurrence. Human relations in industry are today generally stressed in the professional literature, but they are hard to improve when the main effort of the union is to drive employers and employees farther apart, to harp on what it regards as the natural and inevitable conflict of interest between employers and employees, and to make local settlements subject to central policy. . . .

Remedies

No single and effective remedy for the conditions discussed in this study exists, or probably can be found. If Americans desire a change of policy toward organized labor and collective bargaining, they must make up their minds that whatever is done is likely to yield only slow and partial relief. The vested interests created by our national labor policy of the 1930's and by the terms and administration of the Wagner Act are powerful and well entrenched. A property of such inestimable value will not be surrendered without a fight.

One of the most difficult tasks of contemporary society is to recognize the effects of policy and to undo them when they are found to be more harmful than beneficial. Economic and social legislation, once on the statute books, gathers a momentum which carries it far beyond its initial goal. This has been the experience with schemes of social insurance

[1] *Stock and Production Policies in Full-Fashioned Hosiery Manufacture* (Textile Foundation, 1941), p. 15.

in England, Western Europe and the United States. Started as modest undertakings with limited objectives, they soon become among the most important activities of government through the zeal of their public administrators and the pressure of their beneficiaries. As the campaign for extension and liberalization proceeds, little or nothing is said of the increasing burden of costs or of ulterior consequences. In England today, the country's capacity to yield an unusually modest standard of living is in doubt. Yet under pressure from the vested interests in social security the program is being greatly expanded. How the expansion will be paid for, and by whom, appear to be troublesome but irrelevant questions.

We have pursued a similar course with our policies and legislation governing the position and activities of organized labor. Government aid in the unionization of American employees has produced results which few of the supporters of the policy in 1935 would have ventured to predict. To unscramble these results, and to put the policies of labor relations on a basis which will strengthen and not demoralize the American economic system, which will safeguard and not undermine the liberties associated with a free, competitive economy and which will discourage and not promote the intervention of government, would be a formidable task — just as it would prove a formidable task for England to restore private ownership and competitive business, in the event the people of that country decided to reject the Labor Party's policy of a planned economy and nationalized industry.

In this country the die has not yet been cast. American business still discloses a vitality and an ingenuity which distinguish it from British and European business. While a not inconsiderable number of businessmen have been won over to the merits of the "stabilizing" policies of government and organized labor, the great majority of them have consistently opposed these policies because they are convinced that such policies will fail to produce the promised results. With the experience of much of the world before them, there is reason to believe that many American citizens today entertain strong doubts as to the wisdom of the policies they appeared so ready to endorse only a few years ago.

The most urgent and effective means for dealing with the evils which have arisen in labor relations consist in removing the special privileges granted organized labor by government during the last decade. Something has already been accomplished in this direction by the Taft-Hartley Act. Under its terms, employers are placed on a more nearly equal footing with organized labor. Employers are now free to discuss with their employees the pros and cons of organization. The independent, unaffiliated unions are granted something like equality under the law, although there is no assurance that their rights will not be whittled away by decisions of the National Labor Relations Board. It is no longer obligatory for employers to recognize and deal with unions of foremen. Unions, like employers, are required to bargain in good faith. The secondary boycott, whereby unions can attack a business wholly unconnected with the original labor dispute, has been outlawed. As recent occurrences in the coal and railroad industries show, the limited use of the injunction in labor disputes is now sanctioned.

Altogether unsolved is the matter of protecting the right of men to work. Mass picketing has become the accepted method of intimidation in the United States. Small communities, with limited police resources at their disposal, cannot furnish the protection to which their people have a right. State governments are loath to lend assistance because of the fear of political reprisal by organized labor, as events in the recent strike of the meat packers' union clearly showed. To no small extent, the national unions owe their rise to power and their maintenance of that power to the failure of local, state and federal authorities to devise and enforce a fair and equitable policy of law enforcement in labor disputes and of protection of the right to work. If this is not attended to, there will be neither peace nor a sound resolution of the labor problem in American industry.

At bottom, however, the problem of labor monopoly cannot be dealt with effectively unless and until the immunity to the antitrust laws which organized labor has enjoyed since 1914 is withdrawn. This immunity accorded to organized labor by public policy is one of those special privileges of unions which have no reasonable justification. Its perpetuation, in the face of the position organized labor now occupies in making economic policy, will in time cause the breakdown of our entire anti-monopoly policy. This is the first step toward a regulated or planned economy, as it has proved to be in other countries. The English, after many years of inaction and, indeed, of encouragement of business and labor monopoly, are at this late hour becoming alarmed over the evils of monopoly. But a recent bill[2] aimed at monopoly exempts "practices as to the workers to be employed or not to be employed . . . or as to the remuneration, conditions of employment, hours of work, or working conditions of workers."

Any review of American labor condi-

tions and policies should leave little doubt as to the existence of labor monopolistic practices, their effectiveness and the rapidity by which they are being applied to an increasing segment of industry. The opinions of the courts in labor monopoly cases indubitably disclose the existence of monopoly, but they say, as the Supreme Court said in the *Hutcheson* case:[3] "So long as a union acts in its self-interest and does not combine with non-labor groups, the licit and the illicit . . . are not to be distinguished by any judgment regarding the wisdom or unwisdom, the rightness or wrongness, the selfishness or unselfishness of the end of which the particular union activities are the means."

This language is clear enough. It is a fair statement of the character of our public policy toward labor monopoly. It leaves the unions as the exclusive arbiters of their economic decisions. When such decisions produce results contrary to the public interest, there would appear to be no effective means in the law, as it is interpreted today, to protect that interest. When, also, the decisions of unions adversely affect the interests of their members, those members would appear to have no redress "so long as a union acts in its self-interest."

This states the problem of labor policy in the United States today. Is it wise to continue a public policy which has promoted great private combinations of labor, which has granted them a free hand to augment their power and to apply it and which provides no visible means for asserting and protecting the public interest, and with it, the essential interest of laborers — those who belong to unions and those who do not?

2 21 11 & 12 Geo. 6, Sections 3 (2) and 5 (4).

3 *U. S. v. Hutcheson et al*, 3 LABOR CASES ¶ 51, 110, 312 U. S. 219 (1941).

Richard A. Lester: REFLECTIONS ON THE "LABOR MONOPOLY" ISSUE

ESPECIALLY during the last two years, the terms "labor monopoly" and "monopolistic unions" have been widely used in the newspapers, in congressional hearings, in periodicals, and in books. Unfortunately, those who employ the terms, although perhaps citing an example or two of what they have in mind, have not been prone to develop precise definitions or criteria for determining the existence and extent of such monopoly. It is not surprising, therefore, to find statements by economists that seem to be based on different conceptions of "labor monopoly," labor markets, and the nature of labor unions.

Unqualified application to labor markets of a term developed and refined with reference to product markets may be misleading. If practical and workable solutions are to be found for the problem of concentration of power and control in the field of labor, care must be taken to avoid superficial analogies that stimulate name-calling, obstruct real investigation, and cramp analysis within the confines of a preconceived pattern. . . .

The practical importance of a clear and analytical understanding of the problem is indicated by recent congressional hearings and sentiment. In the last Congress, as passed by the House of Representatives, the Hartley bill contained provisions forbidding "monopolistic strikes" and "monopolistic" collective bargaining (defined as involving two or more competing employers except where competing plants were less than fifty miles apart and together regularly employed a total of less than one hundred employees). The Senate defeated, by only a 44-to-43 vote, the Ball amendment to "reduce the concentration of bargaining power,"[1] which would have prevented the National Labor Relations Board from certifying national unions as bargaining agents and would have declared it an unfair labor practice for national unions to bring pressure to bear upon their locals to include or omit any particular terms or provisions in any collective-bargaining agreement. . . .

1. The Nature of Labor Markets

Labor markets differ significantly from commodity or security markets. Each buyer is distinguished from every other buyer and there are as many market places as there are buyers. In the absence of collective bargaining, the buyers quote the wage; research in labor economics generally supports the conclusion that it is normal and natural (in the absence of collective bargaining or employer collusion) for different employers (or even

[1] Senator Joseph H. Ball in the *Congressional Record*, XCIII (April 28, 1947), 4257; also contained in statement of purposes in S. 133 introduced by Senator Ball in the 80th Congress.

Reprinted by permission from *Journal of Political Economy*, LV (December, 1947), University of Chicago Press.

the same employer[2]) to continue indefinitely to pay diverse rates for the same grade of labor in the same locality under strictly comparable job conditions.[3] Adam Smith noted this phenomenon of multiple rates when he wrote: "The price of labour, it must be observed, cannot be ascertained very accurately anywhere, different prices being often paid at the same place and for the same sort of labour, not only according to the different abilities of the workmen, but according to the easiness or hardness of the masters."[4] It is, therefore, erroneous to talk of "pure competition in the labor market," or of "the wage which clears the market," or of "a free labor market [where] different wage rates for the same kind of labor could not long exist."[5]

Not only is a quoted price (wage-fixing) characteristic of the labor market but, unlike commodity or security markets, a considerable degree of stability in wage relationships and in individual wage rates over time is essential for satisfactory employment and manufacturing operations. Perfect fluidity or flexibility in individual wage rates — with frequent upward and downward movements and numerous changes in occupational differentials within a plant — would have adverse effects upon labor efficiency.

2 For such reasons as race, length of service, favoritism, etc.

3 See Lloyd G. Reynolds, *Research in Wages: Report of a Conference Held on April 4–5, 1947* (Social Science Research Council, August, 1947), p. 27; see also my article, "Wage Diversity and Its Theoretical Implications," *Review of Economic Statistics,* XXVIII (August, 1946), 152–59.

4 *The Wealth of Nations* (Everyman's ed.; 1931), p. 69; see also John W. Riegel, *Wage Determination* (1937), p. 8.

5 Economists have insisted both that equal wage rates should be paid in the same locality for identical work regardless of the industry and that there should be a sufficient local differential to attract labor to, and maintain it in, expanding industries.

Such flexibility would be incomprehensible and upsetting to workers, creating all kinds of suspicions and ill will, stimulating undesirable insecurity for employees, and causing wages to be a constant source of friction and speculation.

In the labor market, competition does not establish a single rate for work of the same grade and quality. Real wage differentials exist and persist, in the absence of unions, because of differences in employer policies and because of the nature of the supply of labor.

Employers not only do not wish to vary their wage scales repeatedly but are prone to give general, across-the-board increases or decreases rather than to adjust each rate according to local demand and supply conditions for that occupation. They may not reduce individual rates or the whole scale when they can, or when other local employers are doing so, for fear of the psychological effects on their employees or for reasons of justice, fairness, or conscience. Indeed, the policies of employers toward labor are often in marked contrast to their policies in commodity markets. Many companies seek to lead in wage increases and to pay wages slightly above their competitors. They do not dismiss established employees to hire other labor that may be equivalent or better, even though such labor is offered to the company at wage rates well below the company's current scales. Formal systems of job evaluation, widely used in industry, have no real counterpart in commodity markets. Some multiplant companies pay the same wage scales regardless of the size of city or the region of the country in which their plants are located; others have uniform scales for each zone or region; while others (the majority) try to relate their scales either to those paid by certain other firms in the locality or to rates for the same industry in that area. Some companies tend to raise wages with each increase in the cost of living or to pay employees more per hour or per piece simply because they have been with the company a long time; other companies do not follow such policies. Differences in company wage policies, in employer evaluation of individual jobs, and in stress on various wage factors (including generosity), all contribute to the existence of a range of rates rather than a single rate for any grade of labor in a locality.

Competition also tends to establish real wage differentials because the supply of labor, especially unskilled labor, does not adjust to relative price changes as the supply of individual commodities tends to do. Lower real wages (at least above relief standards) tend to increase the supply of labor offered for sale by a family. Consequently, in the absence of unions, great diversity in wage rates for comparable work has existed in low-wage industries — such as garments and textiles — whose products are sold under market conditions closely approaching pure competition.

Without labor organization, employers tend to dominate the labor market. They establish the price, subject to limits and influenced perhaps by wage leadership. The employer pressure that has been brought to bear against individual companies (such as Ford, Owens-Illinois Glass, International Harvester, and American Telephone and Telegraph) not to upset local wage levels or bid away ("pirate") employees of other local companies is well known. Adam Smith explained the nature of common interest and action of employers when he wrote that they "are always and everywhere in a sort of tacit, but constant and uniform combination"; that "to violate this combination is everywhere a most unpopular

action"; and that little is heard "of this combination, because it is the usual, and one may say, the natural state of things."[6]

The most extreme case of employer domination in the labor market is the buyer's monopoly which exists in company towns, where one company is the sole employer of labor in the "labor-market area." The situation may not be so different where most of the manufacturing labor in a community is employed by two or three large units, often the plants of multiplant companies employing from 25,000 to 350,000 workers. As indicated below, such companies may, through their wage and price policies, be able to stimulate intercommunity rivalry in the sale of labor, to curtail buyer competition in a local market, and largely to eliminate price competition in their product markets through delivered price quotations or other devices.

The Federal antitrust laws have never been applied to labor markets. Employers, as well as workers, have been free to combine and conspire as they might wish in the labor market, which is the only market where industrial firms are all buyers and in which it is practically impossible for sellers to become buyers when prices fall. Nonapplication of the anti-monopoly laws in the labor market is recognition of the fact that, without unions, there are bound to be monopolistic elements in most labor markets and that there are essential differences between price-fixing and monopoly control in product markets and such phenomena as labor agreements, collective bargaining, and strikes by workers.

The nature of the labor market has been explained in such detail because some economists, who have not studied labor markets and employer labor poli-

6 *Op. cit.*, p. 59.

cies, seem to consider employer control under nonunion conditions to be "unsubstantial," "transitory," and "infrequent."[7] They have tended to picture the alternatives as "monopolistic wage determination" by unions or "free [competitive] pricing in labor markets" where unions are absent.[8]

2. The Nature of Labor Unions

Economists sometimes seem to overlook the fact that unions do not "sell labor," are not profit-making institutions, and are as much political as they are economic.

Monopolistic principles developed for

business concerns cannot be applied directly to unions. Unlike companies, unions are not operated to make a profit. Their activities are not determined by comparisons of sales income and costs; their policies are not based on marginal sales revenue, marginal operating costs, or net returns. It is doubtful whether unions consistently attempt to maximize any monetary quantity.[9]

In fact, those who accuse unions of being big and strong monopolies often criticize them for not consistently pursuing monopolistic principles. In seeking and accepting uniform wage scales under national and regional collective bargaining, unions forego the monopolistic practice of charging all that the traffic will bear through discriminatory pricing. In denouncing arrangements for multiple employer bargaining (regional or national in application) as "monopolistic," the House Committee on Education and Labor complains that such arrangements "tend, in some cases, to reduce the resistance of employers to extravagant demands of the unions, and, in others, to holding down wages in plants where greater efficiency than in others might, but for the group arrangements, result in better wages for the employees."[10] Holding down wages is condemned as "monopolistic practices" by unions!

In his famous article on labor monopoly, the late Henry Simons explains how, if he were a union leader, he would "gradually exterminate industry by excessive labor costs" and would "consist-

---

[7] See Henry C. Simons, "Some Reflections on Syndicalism," *Journal of Political Economy*, LII (March, 1944), 7; and Fritz Machlup, "Monopolistic Wage Determination as a Part of the General Problem of Monopoly," in *Wage Determination and the Economics of Liberalism* (Chamber of Commerce of the United States, January 11, 1947), pp. 57–58, 80. Note especially such statements as: "Whatever lack there is in industry's competition for labor can be accounted for either by insufficiencies in the geographical or occupational mobility of labor, or by a lack of employment opportunities during periods of serious employment," and "I know of no evidence of employers' wage-fixing combinations in labor markets in which there were no unions; if there is such evidence, it has not been much publicized." For statements by labor economists emphasizing the practical importance of employer dominance or citing cases of concerted employer control in fixing wages see, e.g., Paul H. Douglas, "Wage Theory and Wage Policy," *International Labour Review*, XXXIX (March, 1939), 342; and Harry A. Millis, "The Union in Industry: Some Observations on the Theory of Collective Bargaining," *American Economic Review*, XXV (March, 1935), 6–7. Economists familiar with employer wage policies during nonunion periods in such industries as steel, oil, or meat-packing or with employer control of labor markets in the South could readily supply "such evidence" to theorists who think in terms of "the competitive wage" as the normal and natural state of affairs when labor organization is absent; see also my *Economics of Labor* (1941), pp. 130–39.

[8] See Simons, *op. cit.*, pp. 22–23; and Machlup, *op. cit.*, p. 80.

[9] For a more extended discussion of the differences between labor unions and business enterprises that appeared after this paper was prepared, see Arthur M. Ross, "The Trade Union as a Wage-Fixing Institution," *American Economic Review*, XXXVII (September, 1947), 566–88.

[10] *Labor-Management Relations Act, 1947* (House of Representatives, 80th Cong., 1st sess., Report No. 245 [April 11, 1947]), p. 36.

ently demand wage rates which offered to existing firms no real net earnings."[11] Consistently following monopolistic theory, he would, through discriminatory pricing, charge all that the traffic would bear.

Unions, however, are political institutions, whose leaders are interested in maintaining their positions and in the growth and reputation of the organization, rather than merely in obtaining a maximum lifetime income for the present membership.[12] Unions seek not only to influence terms of employment but to obtain other goals such as security for the organization, protection of members against arbitrary action by management, and definite limits to the authoritarian system in industry. Consequently, union negotiators may swap a possible wage increase for "union security" or for certain provisions in the grievance procedure. And for reasons of union security and convenience, union leaders may prefer multiple-employer bargaining, which strengthens the economic power of employers (reducing the relative power of the union) and which serves to eliminate the possibility of greater monetary gains to the membership through "whipsawing" — playing companies against one another by bargaining with or striking one at a time.

Most strikes do not occur and continue merely, or even mainly, to obtain the highest net money advantage to the strikers. Economists have pointed out that many strikes have not been in the economic interest of the strikers, citing cases, such as the General Motors strike

in 1945–46, in which "a union imposes on its members a loss of earnings through strike that cannot be made up in less than eight years of work at the wage increases they won through the strike."[13] The psychological, political, and institutional factors in strikes are often much more important than purely monetary considerations. It is completely erroneous to assume that most strikes result because union leaders have not correctly estimated the "employer's concession schedule" and the "resistance schedule" of the workers.[14] As part of a mass movement to emancipate and elevate laboring groups, unions seek to curtail the freedom of management to take arbitrary action toward workers and hope, through written agreements, to gain some measure of democratic self-determination in the workshop.

Union policies, practices, philosophies, and even objectives, have been too diverse to permit any unitary explanation of the labor movement in this country. For example, restrictive policies and practices vary in character and extent with the union and the industry. Craft unions frequently have restricted entrance to the trade, membership in the union, and introduction of labor-saving devices that reduce the demand for craft skill; those practices are not characteristic of industrial unions. As pure craft unions have been declining in relative importance or disappearing, such restrictive practices have been decreasing in general significance. "Make-work" restrictions, including the hiring of unnecessary labor, have also been confined chiefly to

[11] *Op. cit.,* p. 8.

[12] See Sumner H. Slichter, *The Challenge of Industrial Relations: Trade Unions, Management, and the Public Interest* (Cornell University Press, 1947), pp. 129–30.

[13] Machlup, *op. cit.,* p. 50, n. 8.

[14] See J. R. Hicks, *The Theory of Wages,* chap. vii: "The Theory of Industrial Disputes," esp. pp. 141–42 and 146–47. Slichter (*op. cit.,* pp. 129–31) indicates how far actual practice is from theoretical models of collective bargaining.

craft unions and local-market industries, like building, trucking, and amusements.

Restrictions of industrial unions in mass-production industries deal mainly with lay-off and promotion, method of payment, or the techniques of "scientific management." Insistence on seniority and equal treatment regardless of sex or race is to prevent favoritism or discrimination by management. Industrial union policies with regard to methods of payment and management techniques, however, vary considerably. Some unions favor the piece-rate methods; others oppose it. Some favor certain formal incentive systems; others oppose all such systems. Some co-operate with employers in establishing production standards or systems of job evaluation; others refuse to participate, reserving the right to complain and oppose. Industrial unions may oppose increased tempo of operations or additional machine assignments; they may also oppose the setting of arbitrary production schedules or daily stints by workers.[15]

Whether unions serve to increase or decrease the net national product is a nice question. Professor Sumner Slichter has given considerable attention and study to the matter. In a chapter on "The Effect of Trade Unions on the

Management of Business Enterprises" in his recent book, he points out that "many rules introduced into shops by collective bargaining [have] increased the net national product"[16] and concludes that "collective bargaining has stimulated more alert and dynamic management and better managerial practices more frequently than it has hampered management and interfered unduly with managerial discretion," so "that in most industries it . . . yields a larger net output than would have resulted from individual bargaining."[17] Not only have restrictions on management's freedom sometimes increased, rather than reduced, total output, but increased wages in low-wage areas as a result of labor organization have frequently helped to increase labor productivity.

Like business organizations, unions in this country have been growing big, and with increasing size has come greater concentration of power and control at the top. National unions have expanded by extension of jurisdiction and organizing activity and by merger until a number of A.F. of L. and C.I.O. unions have from a half-million to a million members and extend over a number of important industries. A natural accompaniment of increased size and operations is concentration of effective power in the hands of top, paid officials. Numerous factors facilitate centralization of functions and authority in unions — growth in the size of companies and the area of competitive production, advantages of central pooling of benefit and strike funds, need for a bureaucracy of full-time officers for efficiency and responsibility in administration, headquarters control over paid organizers and official publications, and so forth.

15 For example, the 1945 agreements of the Federation of Dyers, Finishers, Printers, and Bleachers of America (a department of the Textile Workers Union of America, C.I.O.) with employers in plain dyeing and machine printing and employers in lacquer and flock finishing, contained the following provision: "The Union agrees that every employee shall perform a full day's work. The Union further agrees that the setting of arbitrary production schedules by workers is contrary to the principle of a full day's work and the Union further agrees that appropriate steps will be taken to eliminate any such condition." Some employers reported favorable results from this provision (see R. A. Lester and E. A. Robie, *Wages under National and Regional Collective Bargaining* [Princeton University: Industrial Relations Section, 1946], p. 66).

16 *Op. cit.*, p. 34.

17 *Ibid.*, pp. 69, 72–73.

With expanding union strength and concentration of control, the problem of the potential power of union officials over large sections of the nation's economy has become more and more serious, especially when that power is used for selfish or political purposes. Unions not only profess to be representative, democratic organizations but historically are part of a protest movement against autocracy in industry. Consequently, expansion of unions into industrial empires, subject to arbitrary exercise of central authority, raises the question of need for curbs to the area of control by a single union and to concentration of functions and power within unions.[18]

3. Meaning of "Labor Monopoly"

Perusal of recent writings and statements indicates that the terms "labor monopoly" and "union monopoly" carry a variety of connotations and meanings. Some writers stress the purpose of unions as the controlling factor; some point to means (certain specified union activities or legislative policies) as the test; to others the economic effects are the criterion for judging the existence of "labor monopoly"; while still others emphasize personal power as the prime consideration.

On the basis of purpose alone, unions have been termed "monopolistic." For example, the Counsel of the National Association of Manufacturers asserts: "It must be recognized that labor unionism is, by its very nature, essentially monopolistic."[19] In much the same vein, Professor Charles O. Gregory has written: "Now labor unionism is a frankly monopolistic and anti-competitive institution, even if its major undertakings have been carried on and justified in the name of competition."[20] Professor Fritz Machlup has stated: "It is the chief purpose of a trade union to obtain monopolistic advantages for its members."[21] Such views would seem to make "labor monopoly" and labor union practically synonymous terms.[22]

In stressing union action and legislative provisions, some economists point to exclusive bargaining rights or to combined action as the essence of "labor monopoly." Thus, Professors Harley L. Lutz and Leo Wolman criticize as "monopoly" the certification of a union as exclusive bargaining agent under federal legislation.[23]

---

[18] For an analysis of the problem of concentration of control in unions by an official of the International Ladies' Garment Workers' Union, see Will Herberg, "Bureaucracy and Democracy in Labor Unions," *Antioch Review*, III (fall, 1943), esp. pp. 407–13.

Anthony Ramuglia, an organizer for the Textile Workers Union of America and for many years a member and officer of the Amalgamated Clothing Workers of America, has recently written regarding "Democracy in the Unions" as follows: "Most of our international unions operate on the level of the cities' political machines. We have in our unions the counterparts of the Hagues, Pendergasts, Vares, Penroses, etc. In many of our unions the democratic processes are as much a mockery as in the sectors of our nation just referred to. In some unions there is even no pretense of democracy. In others there is some finesse in the exercise of dictatorial powers. However, the whole movement is top heavy. The plague of concentrated powers is as general in the CIO as it is in the AFL." (*Labor and Nation*, III [July–August, 1947], 41).

[19] *Labor Relations Program, Hearings on S. 55 and S. J. Res. 22 before the Committee on Labor and Public Welfare* (U. S. Senate, 80th Cong., 1st sess. [March, 1947]), Part IV, p. 1807.

[20] *Labor and the Law* (1946), p. 418.

[21] *Op. cit.*, p. 54.

[22] Professor Jacob Viner refers to "labor monopolies, which is just another term for 'strong' trade unions" (see "The Role of Costs in a System of Economic Liberalism," *ibid.*, p. 24).

[23] See Lutz, "Wages, Profits and Prices," *Commercial and Financial Chronicle*, CLXIII (January 3, 1946), 43–44; and Wolman, *Hearings on S. 55 and S. J. Res. 22*, Part I, p. 100.

To other economists, the fact of combined action (and therefore collective bargaining or the strike per se) is "monopolistic," apparently regardless of purpose.[24] Presumably, therefore, the threat to strike, or its execution, to prevent discrimination in wages among employees by race or sex or to protest against arbitrary management action, say, in discharges or lay-offs would be as "monopolistic" as a strike for the closed shop.[25] To others, union activities or collective bargaining really become "monopolistic" when they cover jointly two or more employers,[26] and especially when the bargaining or strike includes a whole industry or a whole national union.[27]

"Industry-wide" bargaining per se is often condemned as "patently monopolistic" or "the essence of monopoly in labor relations."[28] Senator Irving M. Ives speaks of "the tendency toward monopoly which is apt to be present in nearly every type of industry-wide bargain-

ing."[29] Senator Joseph H. Ball told the Senate in May, 1947: "I myself am convinced from my discussions with various employers although admittedly we did not have any evidence of it in the committee, that industry-wide bargaining is clearly monopolistic."[30] Uncertainty exists, however, as to what is meant by industry-wide bargaining, for that term is often mistakenly used to refer to unilateral nation-wide union action or to wage pattern-setting by negotiations with a few large concerns whose wage leadership the smaller companies are forced to follow. Senator Ball, for example, cited such a pattern-setting case in explaining why he thought industry-wide bargaining was "clearly monopolistic." Cases of real industry-wide bargaining are relatively rare if one means by the term that practically all the industry is represented in a single negotiation.[31]

Most frequently labor unions have been condemned as "monopolies" because of restrictive policies and practices that affect labor output, labor supply, and labor demand. Such policies, mentioned in the previous section, include restrictions on entrance to the job, on individual output, on use of labor-saving methods, on hours of work, and on management efficiency and discipline as well as other "make-work" restrictions, such as insistence on employment of unneeded labor.[32]

---

[24] See John W. Scoville, *Labor Monopolies — OR Freedom* (Committee for Constitutional Government, Inc., 1946), pp. 20–23; and Hastings Lyon, *Dictatorship of the Proletariat in the United States: A Tract for the Times* (1943), pp. 20–23.

[25] Perhaps it is significant, however, that the closed shop is frequently condemned as "union monopoly" but that the same does not hold for seniority or rules regarding the handling of grievances.

[26] See *Hearings on S. 55 and S. J. Res. 22*, Part II, pp. 950, 957.

[27] *Ibid.*, Part I, pp. 115, 118, 484; and Part II, pp. 942, 1015.

[28] See, e.g., statement by Congressman Walter C. Ploeser in *Daily Report on Labor-Management Problems*, No. 138 (Washington: Bureau of National Affairs, Inc., July 6, 1947), p. A-8; and prepared statement of Charles E. Wilson, president of General Motors Corporation, in *Hearings on S. 55 and S. J. Res. 22*, Part I, pp. 484, 540; and John V. Van Sickle, *Industry-wide Collective Bargaining and the Public Interest* (American Enterprise Association, Inc., May, 1947), pp. 13–20.

[29] *Congressional Record*, XCIII (80th Cong., 1st sess. [May 7, 1947]), 4792, 4793.

[30] *Ibid.*, p. 5144.

[31] Railroads and men's clothing are perhaps the prime examples. Professor Van Sickle considers that industry-wide union organization in the bituminous coal industry has changed it from "one of the most competitive industries in the United States . . . into a monopolistic enterprise . . ." (*op. cit.*, p. 14).

[32] See, e.g., Viner, *op. cit.*, pp. 24–25; Machlup, *op. cit.*, p. 68; Wolman, *op. cit.*, p. 115; Lyon,

Earlier comment indicated some of the grounds for believing that, on balance, labor organization may result in a net increase in the national product through its beneficial effects on individual workers[33] and management. Also it was pointed out that most of the restrictive practices, and most of the really effective restriction, are to be found in craft unions, especially in local-market industries.

In connection with "restriction of labor supply," it is argued that "fixing monopolistic wage rates by contract" restricts the number of jobs available in the industries concerned and, consequently, the number of workers who find work in those industries.[34] To Henry Simons, workers, through unions, were "organized to price their services monopolistically," and so he could "see no way to avoid severely restrictive policies save by depriving them [unions] of control over wages, i.e., of bargaining power." Thus to him the issue was "simply whether wage rates should be determined competitively or monopolistically."[35] The same notion is expressed even more forcefully by John W. Scoville, former economist of the Chrysler Corporation, as follows:

General Motors must pay the market price for copper, for steel, and for labor. For if it pays less than the market price, it will be short of materials and be short of workmen. But the United Automobile Workers' Union is not willing that its members receive the market price of labor, for workers can secure the market price without any collective action.

The purpose of the labor union monopoly is the same as the purpose of every other monopoly. The monopoly is formed to get a price above the market price.[36]

The preceding discussion of labor markets indicates how unrealistic and erroneous is such commodity-market reasoning as applied to labor markets. Prior to labor organization in General Motors, the company was the dominant or largest employer in a number of the localities where its plants were operating. General Motors quoted the wage scales that it would pay and enjoyed a significant range of discretion in fixing and modifying such wage quotation. With real wage differentials prevailing as a normal condition in the absence of employer cooperation or union organization it is fanciful to talk of "*the* market price of labor" in a labor-market area. Without unions, labor markets are subject to employer "influence over price," which, by commodity-market reasoning, is considered to be one of the two "essential criteria of monopolistic position" — the other being "control of supply."[37]

The chimerical nature of "*the* competitive wage" becomes evident when an attempt is made to set forth a definition or criterion by which, in concrete cases, to "answer the question whether a particular wage rate is or is not 'monopolistic.'"[38] Professors Simons and Machlup

---

op. cit., pp. 81–82. Professor Lyon goes so far as to condemn the Fair Labor Standards Act and the Social Security Act as "monopolistic" because they serve to reduce the total hours of labor offered for sale (*op. cit.*, pp. 97, 101, 103, 107).

[33] The beneficial effects of labor organization on labor productivity in low-wage areas, such as sections of the South, deserve serious and systematic study. The importance of preventing the vicious circle of poverty breeding poverty is indicated by Professor Viner, *op. cit.*, pp. 28–29.

[34] See Machlup, *op. cit.*, p. 69.

[35] *Op. cit.*, pp. 25, 9, 23.

[36] *Op. cit.*, p. 155.

[37] Machlup, *op. cit.*, p. 55. Actually, control over price would seem to be the only essential criterion.

[38] *Ibid.*, p. 70.

both propose as the crucial test the existence or nonexistence of real wage differentials. If a wage differential exists so that many qualified workers would prefer to be employed in an occupation, firm, or industry but cannot obtain the preferred employment for lack of job openings, the wage rates are considered to be "excessive" and "monopolistic."[39] To quote Professor Machlup, "If many, however, would like to shift but find that no more workers are wanted at the places which pay the better wage, then the better wage is not the result of a naturally scarce supply but of monopolistic wage determination."[40]

Judged by such a test, "monopolistic wage determination" and "monopolistic distortions in the wage structure" were widely prevalent in industry prior to unionization. For example, companies like Standard Oil of New Jersey, Goodyear Tire and Rubber Company, Ford Motor Company, International Harvester Company, and Botany Worsted Mills paid wage scales 10–20 per cent above their competitors during the 1920's. Many qualified workers would have preferred to work for those concerns but could not do so with limits to the total number of jobs available in such companies. The same has been true for high-paying firms in nonunion areas in the South. As previously explained, companies do not, in the absence of unions or employer understandings, pay "equal wage rates for identical work" in a locality. Economists indicate their lack of understanding of labor markets and policies when they assert that "different wage rates for the same work in different industries . . . are economic foolishness."[41]

[39] See Simons, *op. cit.*, p. 14; and Machlup, *op. cit.*, pp. 69–71.
[40] *Op. cit.*, pp. 70–71.
[41] Machlup, *op. cit.*, pp. 65–66.

In the next section an attempt is made to compare union and nonunion wage scales in a number of industries and to compare wage levels under national bargaining with the general level of wages in industry. As the discussion there indicates, the statistics are not adequate for close comparisons or unqualified conclusions. However, they throw doubt on the contention that, through monopoly, labor organizations exact "excessively high" wages or that national bargaining necessarily results in higher levels of wages than local bargaining or unilateral employer determination.

Although it cannot be conclusively demonstrated by statistics, there can be little doubt that the spread of unionism since 1932 has tended to reduce the amount of "unjustified" differentials in wage rates (a) between occupations within a plant, (b) between plants in the same locality, (c) between manufacturing industries, and (d) between areas and regions. Union insistence on "equal pay for equal work" and the stimulus to job evaluation from labor organization — admittedly with some assistance from wartime scarcity of labor and War Labor Board policies — has resulted in the elimination of many intraplant and interplant "wage inequities." Consequently, the wage structure in American industry now is probably less "distorted" than it was in all nonunion industry during the 1920's. At least that is the opinion of a number of industrialists who are in a good position to make such a comparative judgment.

The application of a uniform wage scale throughout an industry, whether by industry-wide bargaining or union-wide enforcement of standards, has been called "complete monopoly" and "monopoly pure and simple,"[42] on the grounds that

[42] See remarks of Senator Joseph H. Ball and

such a wage scale is not adjusted to "the competitive wage level" in each locality and that it eliminates wage competition in the whole industry.

If uniformity in wage scales throughout the country is monopoly, then a number of multiplant firms — such as Ford and Libbey-Owens-Ford — were guilty of such monopoly prior to union organization in the 1930's, having for decades followed a policy of paying the same wage scale wherever their plants were located.[43] The same has been true for civil service jobs with the United States government.

The analogy to commodities is not usually carried over in this respect. For hundreds of industrial products, companies quote uniform delivered prices on a national basis so that purchasers pay the same price regardless of locality or region. Many other products carry uniform delivered prices by zone or region.[44] Prices of such items have not varied with

Senator Robert A. Taft *Hearings on S. 55 and S. J. Res. 22*, Part III, pp. 1191, 1578–79; see also Part II, p. 642.

[43] In reply to a questionnaire in the spring of 1945, six out of forty-eight interregional concerns — one in each of six industries — reported that they paid the same wage scales in their southern plants as in their northern or western plants. See the author's article, "Diversity in North-South Wage Differentials and in Wage Rates within the South," *Southern Economic Journal*, XII (January, 1946), 239.

[44] Products with uniform national or regional prices include branded items in such lines as rubber tires and tubes; drugs and cosmetics; household electrical equipment; advertised foods and groceries; cigarettes, cigars, and smoking tobacco; shoes; men's suits and furnishings; mattresses; some chemicals; national brands of prepared paints; plumbing fixtures; insulation board; many planing-mill products; wire; aluminum; some automobile parts; typewriters, calculating machines, and similar office equipment; business furniture; paper and newsprint; items of hardware like hand tools; turbines and switchgear; industrial motors and controllers; certain "catalogue items" of machinery; portable air compressors; food machinery; saws and saw tools;

local demand and supply, with differences in freight costs from the producing plant, or with differences in local operating costs including retail delivery. Through various pricing devices, employers are able to achieve unity with regard to price and practically eliminate price competition.

It is no doubt advantageous to a multiplant company to follow a policy of geographic price uniformity in order to reduce price competition among sellers in its product markets, a policy of paying prevailing local wage scales in order to reduce price competition among buyers in local labor markets, and a policy of stimulating price competition on the seller's side of the labor market, especially intermarket rivalry. The policy of company adherence to local prevailing wage rates permits buyer co-operation to aid in local wage uniformity and to discourage competitive upbidding of local wage scales while encouraging intercommunity rivalry in the selling of labor. By quoting the price in both commodity and labor markets, manufacturing firms have often been able to take advantage of any monopolistic elements in their position in each market.

Critics argue that industry-wide uniformity in wage scales tends to curtail employment expansion in low-wage areas, citing such industries as the rubber-tire and -tube industry.[45] Tires and

hydraulic lifts; chains, gears, and transmission machinery; water pumps; gasoline service pumps; and electric arc welding equipment; see, e.g. Saul Nelson and Walter G. Keim, *Price Behavior and Business Policy* (Temporary National Economic Committee, "Monograph No. 1" [Senate committee print] [Washington, 1940]), pp. 286–345; and Vernon A. Mund, "The 'Freight Allowed' Method of Price Quotation," *Quarterly Journal of Economics*, LIV (February, 1940), 232–45.

[45] See Van Sickle, *op. cit.*, pp. 11–12; see also Simons, *op. cit.*, pp. 10–12.

tubes carrying the well-known brand names have a uniform price all over the United States, yet the cost of production of tires and tubes in southern plants apparently has, on the average, been lower than in northern plants, for the large companies report that wage rates for all comparable jobs have been 20–30 per cent below the rates in northern plants, and some companies also report that labor efficiency and actual labor output in their southern plants has equaled that in their northern plants.[46] Pricing on an f.o.b., plant-by-plant basis (cost plus reasonable profit) would, therefore, be the effective, competitive method of bringing about expansion in production and employment in the rubber-tire industry in the South. Uniform delivered prices with the producer absorbing the varying freight charges to all destinations and with cost and profits calculated on a company-wide basis may serve to confuse and conceal plant production-cost differences and to retard expansion in the South.

Actually, it is extremely difficult to argue that the price of labor should vary from locality to locality when the worker's tools or equipment, the materials he works on, and the products he makes all carry uniform prices regionally or nationally and when many of the goods he purchases (clothes, foods, household equipment, building supplies, etc.) likewise are sold at uniform prices geographically. Especially is that the case when the reasons given by economists in support of South-North and other geographic wage differentials are found upon in-

vestigation to be weak half-truths and even to be, in some respects, erroneous. For example, Professor Simons writes: "Southern labor, on the whole, simply isn't worth much, to enterprisers or to the community"; "Climate, culture, poverty, and scarcity of complementary resources (especially capital) account for chronically low productivity."[47] Actually, interregional and intraregional wage structures, and the effects of elimination or reduction of wage differentials, are far more complex than such statements would imply. For example, the wage scales of many southern firms and some southern industries averaged as high as (or higher than) their northern counterparts prior to unionization in the South; wage differentials in single labor-market areas in the South are sometimes greater than real South-North industry differentials; and a majority of interregional manufacturing concerns and industrial engineers report labor efficiency and output as high (or higher) in their southern plants as in their northern plants. Additional factual data contradict other conventional assumptions of theorists, but space limitations permit only reference to the material.[48]

Much of the recent complaint against "labor monopoly" seems to be based on the trend toward concentration of economic power in the hands of the leaders of large national unions and the claim that, through "control over employees in great industries," they dictate the terms which must be met if such industries are to continue to operate.[49] Thus, employers

---

[46] See my articles, "Diversity in North-South Wage Differentials and in Wage Rates within the South," *Southern Economic Journal*, XII (January, 1946), 240; and "Effectiveness of Factory Labor: South-North Comparisons," *Journal of Political Economy*, LIV (February 1946), 66.

[47] *Op. cit.*, pp. 10, 11.

[48] The summarizing article is "Southern Wage Differentials: Developments, Analysis, and Implications," *Southern Economic Journal*, XIII (April, 1947), 386–94.

[49] See statement of Professor Leo Wolman, *Hearings on S. 55 and S. J. Res. 22*, Part I, pp.

and congressmen express alarm at the "monopolistic power" of "the top labor leader"; at "the heavy concentration of economic power and actual monopoly of the supply of labor in the hands of a few unions and their leaders"; at "the rank monopoly" involved in "the domination or dictation" from national headquarters; at "a great monopolistic union controlling the total labor supply in an industry"; and at some union leaders' "power to put great masses of people out of work."[50] It is Dr. Florence Peterson's opinion that "those who speak of union monopoly usually think in terms of a strongly entrenched clique of union officers who, because of compulsory membership requirements, are enabled to exercise despotic power over workers and employers alike."[51]

Increasing concentration of economic power in the hands of individual union officials or groups of officials, and the possibilities for arbitrary or imprudent use of such power, raise some real problems for a political democracy and a relatively free, market economy. Involved are such issues as the size and industrial jurisdiction of a national union, the distribution of power and functions within a national union, the extent and operation of the democratic process within the national union, and the possibilities of joint collusion under national or industry-wide bargaining.

In considerable measure, the problem is one of checks and balances rather than simply one of monopoly in the strict sense of that term. Merely to condemn

as "monopoly" almost every well-established practice of trade-unions serves, therefore, to confuse, rather than to shed light on, the significant issues. Nor, in analyzing the problem, does it help to base one's reasoning on misleading and mistaken notions such as that wage-fixing and wage stability are economically undesirable, that all elements of monopoly can and should be eliminated from the labor market, or that unions seek to price labor so as to gain all possible monopoly advantage. Data in the next section seem to indicate that unions have not affected wage rates so much as is generally assumed or in the manner that reasoning on monopoly principles would lead one to believe.

4. Wage Comparisons

Statements concerning the effects of unions on wage scales and wage structures have often seemed somewhat contradictory. Some economists have contended that unions, by means of their bargaining power, have pushed wage scales too high in organized firms, occupations, and industries, thus causing "monopolistic distortions" in the wage structure. Other economists have pointed out that, in a number of industries, wage scales in unionized plants have averaged no higher than in nonunion plants; that hourly earnings or wage levels in unionized industries have not increased relative to nonunion industries over periods as long as four or five decades; and that during the last three or four decades wage scales and hourly earnings under national bargaining in manufacturing industries have not been higher, and have not increased more rapidly, than for manufacturing as a whole.* . . .

112, 115, 116; and Senator Joseph H. Ball, *Congressional Record*, XCIII (1947), 5145.

[50] See *Hearings on S. 55 and S. J. Res. 22*, Part II, pp. 684–85, 686, 935, 1016, 1068. Strictly speaking, a "monopoly of the supply of labor" is possible only in a slave economy.

[51] *Survey of Labor Economics* (1947), p. 640.

* [Lester's data comparing union and non-union wages is omitted. See, however, p. 86. Ed.]

Limitations of the data preclude sweeping generalizations about the effects of unions, or of national and industry-wide bargaining, upon wage scales and wage structures. The available material does not, however, support the assumption that unions act in the labor market as a monopolist would in a commodity market, or that more rivalry between unions would lead to lower rather than to higher wages. One reason that wage rates could remain relatively low for long periods of time under national bargaining in some manufacturing industries is that such bargaining arrangements increase the security of the union and its leaders. Under certain circumstances, industry-wide bargaining or union-wide action might, of course, result in relatively rapid wage increases and comparatively high wage scale. Especially is that likely to be true where rival union centers and dual unions exist, with competition between union officials for leadership, prestige, and personal position.

5. Some Proposed Remedies

Suggested programs for curbing or eliminating "labor monopoly" vary with the authors' diagnosis of the difficulties to be remedied — their definition of "labor monopoly" and their conception of the labor market and of labor unions. Corrective proposals will differ radically depending on whether one envisages "labor monopoly" as exclusive labor representation, as union restrictive policies, as wage-fixing over wide areas, or as concentration of power and control.

Basically, one's concepts and objectives determine the character of his remedial proposals. An author who conceives of the labor market as essentially the same as a commodity market and the labor union as essentially analogous to a business enterprise producing and selling commodities will apply commodity-market reasoning to labor unions and attempt to make labor markets conform more closely to organized commodity or security markets. Assuming that labor unions are on all fours with business monopolies, he is likely to propose strict application of commodity-market principles and legislation (such as the antitrust laws) to labor-union activities. On the other hand, one may conceive of the labor market as subject to its own peculiar principles and conditions, which normally and necessarily involve price-fixing and monopolistic elements, and view labor unions as political institutions, striving to survive, expand, and gain certain positions within a labor movement. Such a conceptual framework rejects the blanket borrowing of commodity-market programs intended to curtail monopoly or enforce competition and requires that any remedial programs be tailor-made for the labor market and labor unions.

The remainder of this paper will examine, first, recommended actions based on commodity-market reasoning and, then, some proposals designed especially for labor unions, which have been offered by congressmen and union officials. The discussion of each proposal must, because of space limitations, be rather brief.

One proposal, based on commodity-market reasoning, is that "competitive bidding" by labor unions be substituted for exclusive "monopoly of bargaining" granted under federal legislation to the union gaining majority representation. Professor Harley L. Lutz, for example, would have employers as free to bargain in the purchase of labor as they are in buying commodities, selecting the supplier currently offering the best terms. On the assumption that unions are suppliers of labor, he would arrange it so that "an employer, having failed to reach an agreement with one group of workers as to wages or other matters of employment, [would] be free to invite some other group to enter into negotiations with a view to arriving at mutually agreeable terms. . . ."[52] With slavery illegal, however, unions are not suppliers of labor in the sense that producers or merchants are suppliers of commodities.

Any such attempt to utilize "competitive bidding" between unions, with the employer free to choose among all offering unions, would stimulate interunion strife and strikes, with the recent evils of union rivalry increased many fold. Moreover, the proposal overlooks the essential differences between practices in labor and commodity markets and neglects the psychology of employees and employers. Workers value job security and employment stability; either seniority under the proposal would be meaningless and programs for employee advancement disrupted, or workers would have to shift from union to union at the will and interest of the employer. Companies value employee loyalty and employee knowledge of the company's jobs and policies. In encouraging frequent group turnover of labor, the proposal not only disregards company investment in employee training but also the other factors that cause employers to operate in the labor market differently than they do in purchasing and selling commodities.

A proposal that has won support by its superficial plausibility is that the antitrust laws be applied to "labor monopolies" in the same way that they are utilized to curtail "industrial monopolies."[53]

Underlying such a recommendation is an assumption that it would be in the public interest to have labor markets conform as closely as possible to the pattern of organized commodity or security markets.

The proposal to subject labor markets and labor unions to the antitrust laws overlooks the fact that the market is not a satisfactory apparatus for solving many labor problems — the optimum hours of work, working conditions, child labor, job security, workers' grievances, and other human aspects of labor relations.[54] Employee and union rivalry and suits at law may be detrimental, rather than helpful, to labor productivity and labor relations. Labor and management are not competitors in the sense that producers of the same commodity are competitors; nor should unions be considered, or be forced, to be rivals in the manner of competing firms.

The antitrust laws do not define "monopoly" or "restraint of trade," nor does the Sherman Act set forth any definite criteria for determining their existence. Do unions restrain trade when they restrict employers by seniority rules, grievance procedures, definitions of normal working hours and holidays, and all the other nonwage provisions of the typical labor agreement? The restriction is not on consumers who, as pointed out above, may enjoy a larger output as a result of union restrictions on management. Do such practices as wage-fixing, domination of a labor market by a single employer, or agreement on labor-market policies by employers constitute "monopoly," which would subject employers to penalties under the proposed extension of the antitrust laws? How would the extent of injury, for which treble damages

[52] *Ibid.*, pp. 43, 44.

[53] See, e.g., Harold W. Metz and Meyer Jacobstein, *A National Labor Policy* (1947), pp. 91 and 159; *Hearings on S. 55 and S. J. Res. 22*, Part I, p. 541, and Part II, p. 686.

[54] For further discussion see my *Economics of Labor* (1941), pp. 39–45.

can be collected under the Sherman Act, be calculated and assessed by the courts if collective bargaining and some of the provisions of typical labor agreements, including wage-fixing, were considered in violation of the antitrust laws? Presumably Senator Robert A. Taft had some of these questions in mind when he stated: "You would practically have to write an anti-trust law for labor, because I do not think the Sherman Act is really aimed at it, or that the wording is particularly suitable."[55]

The fact is that the antitrust laws and litigation under them have proved costly, ineffective, and ill-adapted for the determination and solution of monopoly problems. Court cases drag on for as long as ten years. Court victories usually are only moral victories; companies adjudged guilty can try other means, and generally there is no follow-up after the court decision. Through pricing and costing systems, common conventions, or other means of obtaining accord, firms in an industry can achieve unity of action with respect to price without any conversations or correspondence such as would be necessary in the case of labor because of the numbers involved and the characteristics of the labor market. For such reasons, the antitrust laws have proved to be impotent to prevent the growth of large industrial empires and increasing concentration of economic power in American industry.[56] Extension of the antitrust laws to labor markets, in the face of their unsuccessful record in the field for which they were designed and in view of the essential differences

between labor and commodity markets, would certainly not be sensible.

During the past year or two, a number of special limitations on labor unions have been recommended for congressional action. One type of proposal — embodied in the Hartley bill as passed in the House of Representatives in April, 1947, and also in the Ball bill (S. 133) considered by the Senate — would restrict collective bargaining to a single operating company or to one local labor-market area and would enforce independence of union policy and decision on a company or community basis.[57] Collective bargaining could encompass the employees of two or more employers only if the firms included had a combined total of no more than, say, one hundred employees and were all located in the same trade area or no more than fifty miles apart.

The stated objectives of such proposals are "to prevent monopolistic concentrations of bargaining power," to eliminate bargaining by national unions, to insure complete freedom of action by local unions, to secure more employer-employee participation in collective bargaining, and to forestall industry-wide shutdowns. Careful consideration indicates, however, that the proposed legislation is not well designed to achieve some of the avowed objectives and would not be in the public interest.

Since the restrictions are to be applied only to labor unions and not to employers or employer organizations, they seem patently unfair. One of the fundamental objectives of labor organization, unity of action on wages over the whole area of competitive production of an article,

---

[55] *Hearings on S. 55 and S. J. Res. 22*, Part IV, p. 1793.

[56] For a good discussion of the weaknesses of our antitrust laws and machinery see Walton Hamilton and Irene Till, *Antitrust in Action* (Temporary National Economic Committee Monograph No. 16 [Washington, 1940]).

[57] In addition to congressional bills and discussion see, e.g., Raleigh W. Stone, "Trade Unionism in a Free Economy," *University of Chicago Law Review*, XIV (April, 1947), pp. 406–7.

is forbidden, but no corresponding restriction is proposed with respect to unity of action on the price of the article over the whole competitive area. If "employer" were substituted for labor organization in these proposals, such employer practices as exchange of wage information, use of a common consulting service, discussion at employer meetings, or even casual conversation or correspondence would presumably be considered illegal if they resulted in two or more companies (of any size or in separate communities) adopting any particular wage, hour, or other labor policy.

This type of recommendation is radical in the extent to which it would alter the character and structure of labor unions as they have existed here and abroad for as long as one hundred and fifty years. National unions would presumably become ineffectual federations, leaving the labor movement top-heavy with loose associations — some one hundred and sixty present national unions in addition to the existing duplicate sets of national, state, and local (A.F. of L. and C.I.O.) federations. Craft unions would be most severely affected, since they are organized by occupation rather than employer; even some existing craft and industrial locals would have to be divided.[58] Without a thoroughgoing breakup of industrial combinations and large companies, this sort of proposal seems neither logical nor defensible. There may be little more reason for unions to be cut up according to the odd conglomeration of activities in many of the multiplant companies than there would be for companies to be confined to the jurisdiction of individual national or local unions. A union limited to the

operations of one employer or a few small employers in one community might be too small or distorted for economical and effective operation.

The consequences of such a proposal would not be what proponents indicate. It would foster union rivalry, instability in labor relations, and irresponsibility in organized labor. National unions generally are a restraining influence on local unions, because their officers are farther removed from the scene of conflict, have a broader and longer-run point of view, are more aware of the lessons of past experience, and are more interested in conserving strike funds and retaining their union jobs. To destroy the responsibility of the parent organization, to increase the number of independent unions in manufacturing by five hundred to a thousand times, and to have labor negotiations and changes in the terms of employment occurring in an industry all the time would serve to increase the confusion and turmoil, the labor unrest, the amount of industrial conflict, and the time lost from strikes. Also, compulsory independence of policy-determination would retard the spread of labor practices that the experience of one or more companies showed to be beneficial. In addition, there would be the unfavorable effects on labor relations resulting from the disruption of existing relationships and the bitterness engendered by dissolution of national unions and enforced segregation of the pieces.

It is not clear which of the various meanings of "labor monopoly" the proponents of this type of legislation have in mind as their target. Since the labor market is a local market, confining collective bargaining and policy determination to one "labor-market area" would not necessarily prevent monopoly in that market, either on the demand or on the

[58] See Senator Wayne Morse's remarks in *Congressional Record*, XCIII (80th Cong., 1st sess. [May 7, 1947]), 4798.

supply side. Limitation of the bargaining and collective action to an individual firm might seem to reduce the possibility of monopoly if the industry is not dominated by one or a few large firms and the number of firms is not decreasing. However, individual-firm bargaining favors the large company and may help to reduce the number of firms in existence. To prevent small companies in an industry from gaining the advantages of joint action in collective bargaining (except when they happen to be located in the same community) is to discourage the existence of small companies by exposing them both to pattern-setting in labor matters by the large concerns without consideration of the interest of the smaller firms and to the threat of strike action against one small company at a time. It has been to avoid such weak and unsatisfactory positions that many employers have resorted to multi-employer bargaining, which has been especially prevalent in industries characterized by a hundred or more small firms, with no one firm having as much as 5 per cent of the industry's total output, such as men's and ladies' clothing, women's hosiery, and cotton textiles.

Industry-wide shut-downs have often taken place in industries in the absence of multiple-employer bargaining and can readily occur through the spreading of a strike, regardless of the area included in a single negotiation. Indeed, the manufacturing industries subject to national and regional collective bargaining have been notably free from crippling strikes during the past decade, and some of them have had no authorized strikes since national or regional bargaining was instituted.

The proposal to compel local or company-wide independence of bargaining and union policy raises serious practical problems. The employer unit of organization is especially objectionable where employment is characteristically of short duration, as in the building and maritime industries and in some canning operations.

Even more difficult would be the problems of effective enforcement. To prevent national unions from playing any role in union policy formulation or determination and to compel independence of union policy by company or community, it would presumably be necessary to make it an "unfair labor practice" or illegal for national union officials to make statements on union policy or to print suggestions for union demands, if the granting or withholding of the use of the national union's support, insignia, funds, or favors were implied in any way. Therefore, enforcement would seem to require significant curtailments of freedom of speech and the press as well as a marked degree of government intervention in the internal affairs of unions. If national officials were trying to bring pressure upon an official or officials of an affiliated local in favor of some policy, the local officials would usually be the only ones directly cognizant of that fact. But they might hesitate to complain, for example, for fear that their progress within the union would be jeopardized thereby. Would the National Labor Relations Board or some other government agency attempt to prevent — for an *indefinite period* through an injunction or cease-and-desist order — the national union from withdrawing its charter to the local, or the national officials from discriminating against a complaining official in promotion? If so, how could the Board assure the complaining official that his opportunities to elective or appointive office in the national union were fully protected at all times? Such questions indicate the real practical difficulties facing any attempt to enforce decentralization of national unions and local autonomy within a political organization that is part of a labor movement, with its own loyalties, traditions, and codes of conduct.

Some union officials have urged enforced "union democracy" and "systematic decentralization of power and devolution of function," reducing the power of top officials of national unions by increasing rank-and-file control.[59] To at-

tempt through legislative enactment and enforcement to control the operation of unions, or even the frequency and nature of elections to union office, would, however, involve governmental interference in the internal affairs of unions that could hardly be justified as an anti-monopoly measure. To promote a broad outlook instead of narrow economic interests and stress on short-run advantages of single unions, Professor Sumner Slichter urges a shift of power and influence from national unions to the two great federations.[60] He does not, however, propose legislation for that purpose. . . .

[59] See, e.g., Herberg, *op. cit.*, pp. 24, 25; *Hearings on S. 55 and S. J. Res. 22*, Part III, pp. 1596–97 and 1625.

[60] *Op cit.*, pp. 175–76.

John V. Van Sickle: INDUSTRY–WIDE COLLECTIVE BARGAINING

INTRODUCTION

INDUSTRY-WIDE collective bargaining is a substitute for individual-plant and local bargaining. The men representing management at the bargaining table speak for all or most of the plants in the industry, the labor representatives speak for all the local unions. Each side has the power to commit its constituents with respect to all of the issues on which they have agreed to bargain collectively. Of these issues the most important is the wage rate.

Industry-wide collective bargaining thus requires common action by all employers in an industry with respect to the largest-single-cost item in their operations. This common action tends to result

in the complete standardization of the rates of pay for the various categories of workers in all the plants in the industry. Standardization cannot always be realized at the outset.[1] But the pressures are all toward standardization. This is inevitable, since plants that are able and willing, or that would in any event be forced to offer unusually favorable terms, want assurances that their competitive posi-

[1] In Sweden, for example, where industry-wide collective bargaining is the general rule, very wide differentials are set by districts based on population densities, with the highest rates in the Stockholm district, but these differentials are being steadily whittled away under trade-union pressure. Similar differentials can also be found in this country, based on recognition of the need of adjusting the terms of individual plant contracts to local conditions.

Statement submitted in Hearings on Economic Power of Labor Organizations, Committee on Banking and Currency, United States Senate, 81st Congress, 1st Session, part 2, pp. 883–891.

tions will not be weakened by collective bargaining. Labor's representatives avowedly press for all that the traffic will bear. Wage standardization is the end goal of industry-wide collective bargaining, and it must be judged on this basis.

As a believer in trade-unionism, I have reluctantly come to the conclusion that this type of bargaining must somehow or other be outlawed before it destroys not only itself but also the institution on which it depends—the private-enterprise system.

America's Stake in Private Enterprise

Much more than unionism, of course, depends on private enterprise. It is becoming daily more and more clear that all our liberties depend upon private enterprise; that peace itself and the survival of western civilization may well hang in the balance. Hamstrung and restricted, private enterprise cannot discharge its immense responsibilities. It is like a motorcycle. It is stable only when it is in motion. It must be vigorous, responsible, competitive, and expansive, or it collapses. Monopoly, which is simply another name for protectionism, is the fatal virus disease that has destroyed the system in one country after another and is rapidly sapping its vitality in this country.

Capitalism Must Be Competitive

Men always have and always will try to protect themselves from competition. The American economy is riddled with protectionist practices. Most of them are made possible by the sins of commission or omission of our legislative bodies. Industry-wide collective bargaining is only one aspect of the larger problem of monopoly. Today, however, it constitutes far and away the most serious single threat to the system simply because

unionism now dominates all our basic industries and because wages constitute so large a part of costs.

Monopoly business profits are ethically as offensive as monopoly wages but they bite less deeply and hence there is always less time for the curative forces within the system to root them out before they do irreparable harm. Rival business groups show extraordinary ingenuity in breaking up one another's monopolies unless Government lends a helping hand.

Great Expectations

Lawmakers, of course, cannot be expected to legislate in the interests of private enterprise unless the people not only want to preserve the system but also understand how it operates. Though the vast majority of us prefer the system to any of the available alternatives, very few of us understand how it operates. This goes for hosts of business and farm leaders as well as union leaders. Meantime the system's enormous and rising productivity[2] has given birth to absurdly exaggerated expectations. Vast numbers have come to believe that they can get today through collective action what the system can easily provide tomorrow. Organized workers see in profits a magic reservoir from which wage advances easily attainable a few years hence can be had here and now. Other pressure groups see in these same profits funds to be tapped by Government in support of social reforms all desirable in themselves, all possible when viewed one at a time, but adding up to totals which are far beyond our means. In our impatience we are killing the goose that lays the golden eggs.

[2] Hourly earnings, as Prof. Sumner Slichter pointed out in the New York Times Magazine of May 18, 1948, rose about eightfold between 1840 and 1940 while the price level remained almost unchanged.

The London Economist of May 1, 1948, remarked that Britain had lived beyond its means between the two world wars, and that now, without a mighty effort at self-analysis and regeneration it might find itself dying beyond its means. Does not the fact that the physical productive equipment of the United States was less in 1945 than in 1931 suggest that we may be travelling the same road? Never before in our history had we failed over an equal space of years to expand enormously the tools and equipment at our disposal. Like Britain, we have been living on our fat.[3]

The Problem of Pressure Groups

Can this ominous trend be reversed? Personally I see little hope unless big pressure groups can be broken down into the little ones that a democratic government can handle. The small pressure group has a constructive role to play. The individual acting alone seldom succeeds in focusing public attention on injustices long enough to get them remedied. He needs the support of a group. Frequently these little groups get more than they are entitled to, as witness the dairy farmers and the heavy oleomargarine taxes and the mountain bloc and our absurd silver purchase program. But the tribute they levy is relatively small and private enterprise can carry the load until a counter bloc wipes out the abuse.

Trade-unions in the United States until recently fell in the category of little pressure groups. They forced management to pay more heed to the human element. They brought home to businessmen the fact that the shop produces men and women as well as commodities. They introduced "due process" into the shop.

They cleared up many an abuse that top management did not even suspect. They gave status to workers, and status, as anthropologists or sociologists will testify, is an essential ingredient of a healthy society.

Unions like every other social organization obey what may be called "the law of diminishing social utility." Industry-wide collective bargaining is an extension of unionism that goes far beyond the limits of tolerance. Many defend it as an appropriate countermove to the giant corporation. This may be good psychology, but it is poor economics. However, in a democracy psychology is as important as economics.

The Problem of Big Business

May I therefore digress for a moment from my main theme and suggest that if business wants to see labor's power splintered it may have to accept some of the same medicine. The privileges accorded corporations need to be reexamined. Is there any sufficient reason why a single corporation should be allowed to produce a wide range of utterly unrelated products and funnel excess profits made in one line into supporting production in other lines? It takes a good deal of courage for newcomers to break into a field if the plants already in operation are affiliated with giant corporations which they can tap for engineering know-how, and for support in a war of extermination against independents.

A private enterprise system loses vitality when entry is fraught with unnecessary risks. For the system to survive a lot of people have got to have a direct and passionate stake in it. A lot of people must be able to say, "This is my business. I built it up and I'll defend it." Wide distribution of stock ownership in a few giant corporations is not an adequate

[3] C. Reinold Noyes, president of National Bureau of Economic Research, in the American Economic Review, March 1947.

substitute. I suspect that substantial changes could be brought about here without any appreciable loss in efficiency, for in most fields the optimum size plant is not enormous. Personally I think the Congress should consider establishing a quantitative definition of monopoly based upon a percentage of the market and substantially lower than the courts have been willing to set. The Federal Trade Commission might be authorized to recommend higher percentages in industries in which the lower percentage would clearly involve a serious loss in efficiency. Tariffs should be drastically lowered on commodities produced by only a few domestic suppliers.

Industry-wide Collective Bargaining Favors Labor Monopoly

But it is time to return to my main thesis, which is that industry-wide collective bargaining should be outlawed as contrary to the public interest.

Collective bargaining in bituminous coal, in rails, and in rubber provide excellent examples of the antisocial effects of this new type of bargaining.

BARGAINING IN COAL

Bituminous coal is found in over half the states of the Union. Ownership is wisely diffused. Inherently the industry is highly competitive. Wages make up more than 60 percent of costs. Hence it is very sensitive to geographical wage differentials. It is also extremely sensitive to transportation charges. In general processing moves toward coal rather than vice versa.

... Industry-wide collective bargaining in coal is clearly not a natural phenomenon. It is a Government-made product. And what are the results?

1. It has converted one of the most competitive industries in the United States into a virtual monopoly and it has turned over to one man the power to close it up and hence to bring the entire economy of the United States to a standstill.

2. It has protected the mine owners and the mine workers in a relatively wealthy area at the expense of the mine owners and all but a privileged minority of the working population in a relatively poor area.

3. It has enabled a privileged group of workers to charge a rate for their services which exceeds that paid to any other large industrial group in the country.

4. It has enabled this same group to take unto themselves all of the benefits of the great technological improvements which have characterized the American coal industry, and which otherwise, because of the inherently competitive nature of the industry, would have been passed on to consumers in the form of lower coal prices.

5. Not content with absorbing the gains of technology the United Mine Workers have exacted further tolls in wages and related benefits. The mine operators can for the time being pass on higher prices to domestic and industrial consumers of bituminous coal. The latter in turn have shifted the costs onward, pyramiding the burden in the process, to end users, the vast majority of whom earn less than the coal miners.

6. Bargaining in coal has created unrest throughout the labor movement. It has forced union leaders in every other industry to demand wage increases regardless of competitive conditions.

7. It has thus been a major influence in getting us into a highly dangerous inflationary spiral.

8. In the event of a depression the downward inflexibility of miners' wages, particularly when controlled by a reso-

lute and powerful union, will result in massive unemployment in the mining industry and the bulk of this unemployment will be concentrated in one of the poorest parts of the country.

BARGAINING OF THE RAILROADS

The antisocial effects of industry-wide collective bargaining are revealed with equal clarity in the case of the railroads. With the aid of this weapon and of repeated threats to close down the roads wage rates were bargained steadily upward throughout the period between the two wars. This happened despite the fact that the roads laid off close to a million men during the same period and that a substantial fraction of the railroad mileage was in bankruptcy. In 1938 the average earnings of railroad employees exceeded those in all other industries by 28 percent and the rates were substantially the same all over the country. During the late 1930's the operating personnel in Southern Territory were actually making more than those in Official Territory because of the longer daily runs. Non-operating employees got slightly less.

Regional Anomalies

These wage uniformities produced strange distortions. In the South Atlantic States the average earnings of railroad employees exceeded those in all other industrial categories by 59 percent; in the East-South Central States by 64 percent. In South Carolina they were 74 percent higher; in Mississippi 87 percent higher. In California on the other hand, they were a shade under the general level.

During the same period commercial trucking and bus transportation grew by leaps and bounds. New workers were recruited by the tens of thousands at substantially lower rates for jobs as exacting as those of railroad workers. Not only were rates lower but they conformed with the pattern of wages in the areas in which they operated.

Had the railroads of the South been permitted to pay rates no greater than those in the expanding and competitive highway transportation industry it is safe to say that the ICC could have given the South the type of freight rates required for its expanding industries. Instead, and under strong political pressure, it made partial restitution by imposing higher class rates on the roads in Official Territory. At present the railroads control neither their freight and passenger rates nor their wage rates and they face severe competition from three quarters — road, air, and water transport — all of which receive generous public aid. Unable to squeeze any more from the railroads union leaders now demand nationalization. This is a device by which they can tap the pocketbooks of the American taxpayers directly and without the need of an unpopular increase in freight rates. If every large industry that fails to satisfy union leaders is to be nationalized the chances of a balanced budget and stable prices will be very slim indeed.

BARGAINING IN RUBBER

Coal and rails illustrate the results that follow when an industry is tied and has to stand and take it. Once the investment is made it is helpless. But what about an industry that is not tied to any particular site; that can move out of an area in which it is discriminated against?

The rubber industry provides a good example of the moderating influence of the migratory capacity of an industry. It also explains why union leaders attach so much importance to industry-wide collective bargaining.

During the 1930's the wages of the rubber workers in Akron, the capital of the industry, were pushed up substantially under union pressure. Akron became known as a high-wage town. The companies met the pressure by concentrating their expansion programs in smaller communities. Their practice was to pay slightly better than the highest wages prevailing in these communities for the types of labor they required. Even so, they were well below the Akron level. Akron's future was threatened and with it the future of the union. In 1937 the union countered by levying an assessment of 2½ cents per worker per month "to organize the hinterland." In 1940 the assessment was raised to 5 cents.

The alleged purpose of the organization drive was to stop what was claimed to be the exploitation of the rubber workers in the hinterland. The real purpose, of course, was to bring the industry back to Akron. Neither the leaders nor the rank and file were concerned about the consumer. Consumers as such have no special interest in riding on tires made in Akron. If tires can be made at a lower money cost in smaller communities, consumers will sooner or later get their tires at a lower price and will buy more tires or have more money to spend on other things. Lower prices mean more jobs for rubber workers. Stopping expansion in smaller communities by forcing rubber factories there to pay wages well above the prevailing rate thus blocks price reductions, reduces the total number of jobs in the industry, and particularly reduces the number of well-paid jobs in the smaller communities — as judged by local standards — and piles up the numbers competing for the lower-paying jobs available in these communities. Thus good jobs in terms of available alternatives are destroyed in the precise places

and the precise industries where they are most needed. Advocates of industry-wide collective bargaining see Akron's gain. What they fail to see is the consumer's loss and the new jobs that fail to materialize.

THE INDICTMENT

Industry-wide collective bargaining is bad economics, bad ethics, bad sociology, and bad politics.

It Is Bad Economics

Industry-wide collective bargaining is bad economics first and foremost because it tends to convert an industry into a monopoly regardless of how inherently competitive the industry may be. The individual firms, confronted with a single bargaining agent, have no choice but to associate themselves firmly together to resist the pressure. At the bargaining table the small firms in the smaller communities are inevitably sacrificed to the need of a settlement. The industry gets concentrated into a few large concerns located in the larger centers. For these concerns it is but a small step from co-ordinating their wage costs to coordinating their prices and allocating the market. A cartel is in the making. The next step is as easy as it is inevitable. The labor cartel and the management cartel get together, and sink their clasped hands deep in the pocketbooks of consumers. Prices, profits, and wages in different segments of the economy part company. Neither the labor nor the capital caught in less remunerative fields can come to the rescue of consumers. A joint management-labor cartel is the last word in monopoly. Only competition from outside the national frontiers could force these monstrosities to compete, but a people and a government that deny to their own domestic capital and labor the right to compete will certainly not let foreigners do so.

Every industry in which the terms of employment are fixed by industry-wide collective bargaining now becomes affected with a public interest. Nation-wide shut-downs now become at once possible and intolerable. The leaders on the management side, it is true, would not dare shut up shop because the owners can easily be fined and brought to heel, but can the same be said of the leaders on the labor side? European experience and our own experiences during and since the last war provide the answer. A country which accepts industry-wide collective bargaining as the key to industrial peace turns over the control of the economy, the very existence of the society, to a small and powerful group of labor leaders who have risen to leadership by processes outside the control of the people as a whole and whose responsibility is sectional and partial.

A private enterprise economy operating under the handicap of industry-wide collective bargaining simply cannot "deliver the goods." Public opinion cannot be expected to rally to the symbols dear to the believers in private enterprise when these have lost all resemblance to reality.

The pressure for industry-wide collective bargaining comes from unions and plants in highly urbanized areas where the slow natural growth of population and the rapid growth of investment funds force employers willy-nilly to pay relatively high wages. These high wages, though needed to recruit labor, naturally induce some of the investment funds and such plants as are unable to pay these wages, to shift to smaller and more rural communities, where lower wage rates prevail. These lower rates result from the fact that local investment funds are less

abundant and the labor supply more abundant due to the high natural rate of population growth in the surrounding agricultural area. The wage differential offsets the disadvantages of distance from end-markets thus making possible the profit differential essential to the development of smaller communities. The two differentials set in motion complicated but highly desirable cross movements of labor and capital. Surplus workers are continuously moving to cities. Some move to the nearby smaller communities, trying out jobs there before deciding to make the final break with farming. Others make a clean break with the farm and go directly to the big metropolitan centers, lured there by the higher wage rates. Sometimes the move is by stages. On the other hand profit differentials redistribute to smaller communities part of the investment funds formed in or drawn to the great metropolitan centers by the presence there of the great financial institutions.

This is the essence of the area competition which has helped keep our economy flexible and dynamic despite the innumerable monopoly abuses to which it has been exposed. Industry-wide collective bargaining strikes a deadly blow at this kind of competition. In effect it vetoes the movement of capital toward the areas which are producing the labor supply. It insists that men shall move to existing job centers whereas the price mechanism in a genuinely competitive economy divides the burden more equitably between labor and capital.

This kind of collective bargaining penalizes the farm population in two ways. It makes more difficult the transfer to nonfarm jobs of the surplus workers continuously produced by our biologically robust farm population. It promotes chronic agricultural over-production, soil mining, low farm prices and low farm incomes. The barter terms of trade between farmers and nonfarmers are loaded against farmers. Having aided organized labor and monopoly business enterprise to exploit the farmers the Congress then finds itself forced to appropriate billions of dollars to provide farmers with an artificial substitute for the genuine and self-supporting parity which competition tends to produce.

Industry-wide collective bargaining thus lowers total productivity, increases inequalities, and reduces the real purchasing power on which a high employment economy depends.

It Is Bad Ethics

Industry-wide collective bargaining is bad ethics. It protects the strong against the weak, the "haves" against the "have-nots," the big cities against the small communities, the urban population with its substantially higher standard of living against the poorer farm population. It imposes the main burden of adjusting to the requirements of a dynamic economy upon the people in areas where local alternatives are most lacking instead of distributing the burden between men and inanimate capital. As Walter Lippmann put it in his The Good Society, the private enterprise system requires mobility of labor and capital, but "capital should be more mobile than labor." Industry-wide collective bargaining sins against this fundamental ethico-economic principle.

It Is Bad Sociology

Industry-wide collective bargaining is bad sociology. By forcing men to move to big cities it helps create the super-metropolitanism which threatens the very future of our western civilization. The huge city is not favorable to the good

life. In no part of the Western world do the men and women in our big cities begin to reproduce themselves. Mobs and mob hysteria are big city phenomena. The sense of personal insecurity varies directly and progressively with the size of the city. Life is more natural and more relaxed in small and intermediate-sized communities. Widely diffused such communities draw urban and rural folk together in a wholesome relationship that is as sound from the sociological point of view as it is profitable from the economic point of view. Harmonious labor-management relations are much easier to develop and to maintain in small cities than in our huge and congested cities.

A genuinely competitive private enterprise system works constantly to create such a pattern. Left to itself it tends to create wage differentials which vary roughly with community size. These differentials exercise a powerful and socially sound decentralizing influence. It forces a new business contemplating settlement in a big city or an established business contemplating an expansion to figure out carefully whether the very substantial benefits to be gained from close proximity to a rich end-market are sufficient to offset the high costs that attach to doing business in the big city. Thus wage differentials (and rent differentials which also tend to vary with the size of cities) exercise a constant and constructive "screening" function, selecting for communities of different sizes the economic activities best suited to the cost structures associated with size.

If the system is dynamic constant small adjustments are required. These are frequently painful for individuals. The State can and should soften and humanize these adjustments. It can and should aid those exposed to the cross-fires of change. But in doing this care must be taken not to aid the individual by protecting his customary job or by providing him with support on so generous a scale as to relieve him of the responsibility for adjusting to the new situation.

Industry-wide collective bargaining is the natural protective response of labor and established businesses in the big cities to this screening process. Ways and means must be found to break down this protectionism before it destroys the greatest and richest single free trade area in the world.

It Is Bad Politics

Industry-wide collective bargaining is bad politics because it creates a state within a state. Democratic government simply cannot handle effectively such concentrated power.

Confronted with such a situation a people have three choices. They can choose a "man on horseback" or a "man with a mustache" to break the grip of the unions, or they can turn over the government to a labor party and hold it responsible for organizing production, or they can elect representatives and instruct them to remove from the statute books all aids to monopoly.

The first two choices involve an enormous and dangerous expansion of the power of the state. The Government has to be strong enough to master the leviathan pressure groups which its neglect has called into existence. Its bureaucracy must be clothed with powers which are as objectionable in the hands of political appointees as they are in those of pressure group appointees. Those who sponsor either one of these choices should remember that power is always dangerous. No group, no class, no church, no trade association, no professional association, no labor union can be trusted with much power, for, as Lord Acton has pointed out, "power corrupts and absolute power corrupts absolutely."

CONCLUSION AND RECOMMENDATIONS

The single greatest issue today in the field of labor-management relations is union monopoly. This monopoly power must be cut down to the point where the union can exercise its legitimate functions and make use of its legitimate weapon — the strike — without jeopardizing the entire economy. Specifically, as I see it, this means —

(1) That the union must be open — not closed — and open on reasonable terms to all qualified workers;

(2) That the jurisdiction of unions should be limited to local areas;

(3) That the coordination of wage demands by unions in different areas should be as resolutely repressed as any efforts of competitive plants within a single industry to agree upon and to enforce a common price policy;

(4) That law and order and the right to work should be enforced at all times and in all cases.

Edwin E. Witte:

ECONOMIC ASPECTS OF INDUSTRY–WIDE COLLECTIVE BARGAINING

An Institutional Approach

THE impetus for multi-employer bargaining has come at times from the unions and at times from the employers. As was pointed out by the pioneer labor economist, John A. Commons, many years ago, unions, to be effective in raising wages and other major terms of employment, must always strive to control and standardize conditions within the product market area of the industry in which they operate. Unless they are able to do so, they tend to handicap the "fair" employers in their competition with the unorganized plants. The market area for some products and most services is essentially local in character; for other products, a region — often not clearly delimited. For the majority of all manufactured products, however, particularly consumer goods, the market area has become pretty much the entire nation. To operate effectively in such industries, the unions must seek to unionize the entire industry, and it is generally both an economic and a political necessity for them to try to equalize, or very nearly so, wage costs throughout the industry. If nothing else, such a policy is dictated by considerations of union politics. Differences in wage rates produce discontent in the lower-paying establishments and endanger the position of the union leaders in

office. It is natural, also, that where a few large corporations are dominant, as they are in many industries, the unions should feel that they must be equally strong and must control all of the workers in the industry, which leads to their insistence upon company and industry-wide bargaining.

Multi-employer bargaining in numerous instances, however, has developed, not because of union insistence, but as a protective device for employers. Sometimes multi-employer bargaining has come about to overcome union whipsawing tactics. Unions have "picked upon" one employer at a time to force him to make wanted increases or other concessions. Then they have used the concessions won from the picked-upon employers to gain like terms from the rest. It has also been a union practice in multi-employer strikes to make settlements with a few of the managements involved to force the rest into line. Very important in the development of multi-employer bargaining also has been the feeling of small employers that they are over-matched in dealing with powerful international unions. When the history of the multi-employer collective bargaining agreements is run down, it is my belief that it will be found that it was the

Reprinted by permission from *Proceedings of the Conference on Industry-wide Collective Bargaining* (1949), University of Pennsylvania Press.

employers who pressed for such bargaining far more often than the unions. Even regional bargaining was strongly resisted by the railroad managements until in the great depression the railroads needed immediate wage reductions and found the process of negotiating separately for each line and craft to be too slow to help them. So in 1934, at their insistence, national bargaining on the railroads was instituted. Both in textiles and in coal, it was the unionized employers who constantly pressured the unions to organize the South and other unorganized regions. Similarly, it was the San Francisco Employers' Council and the strong waterfront employer organizations which initiated and presently strongly support multi-employer bargaining of the administrative type which has become so important on the Pacific Coast. As Adam Smith noted in *The Wealth of Nations*[1] as long ago as 1776, employers even when there are no unions often act together in fixing wages.

More debatable but reasonably clear is the fact that multi-employer bargaining often has proven advantageous alike to employers and employees. Some evidence to this effect is afforded by the long continuance of many multi-bargaining arrangements. Very few instances can be cited where either side has tried to break up such arrangements or refused to continue with them once they have been established. In the extended hearings which preceded enactment of the Taft-Hartley Act, which were pretty much a forum of employers to air their grievances against the unions, there were many denunciations of industry-wide bargaining, but almost none of them from employers who have had actual experience with multi-employer bargaining.

Offsetting the southern coal operators who expressed their dissatisfaction with having been brought into the same bargaining conferences with the northern operators was the testimony of Pacific Coast employer representatives who vigorously took the position that labor relations had greatly improved under multi-employer bargaining. The same attitude has often been taken by employers in the hosiery and the men's and women's clothing industries and very generally by the building contractors. Similar satisfaction exists in both meat packing and steel with the standardized and simplified wage-rate structures which have been established on a nation-wide basis in these industries since the close of the war, under programs initiated by the National War Labor Board.[2]

The advantages which multi-employer bargaining affords to employers and employees flow, in large part, from the greater stability which it tends to produce where it applies to most of the employment in a labor market area, whether it be local, regional, or national. Such stability is particularly advantageous to the established producers in highly competitive markets, as it tends to take wages out of competition and lessens the menace of the wage-cutter. The chiseler and the runaway shop represent new problems produced by multi-employer bargaining, but these can be controlled through policing of the agreement by

[1] Chapter 8.

[2] Developed by the Meat Packing Commission and the Steel Commission. Clark J. Kerr (with Judge, now Governor, Knous and, later, Pierce Davis, as Co-Chairmen) was the guiding head of the former, and William E. Simkin and Theodore W. Kheel of the latter. Both these commissions were established in 1945 under orders of the National War Labor Board to eliminate wage-rate inequities. Both commissions were continued voluntarily by the parties after the National War Labor Board went out of existence and most of their work was done after that time.

both the employers' association and the union and by the union's following the employers wherever they may locate. Wage standardization tends to reduce labor stealing and labor turnover in times of keen demand for labor and to protect the workers against competitive wage-cutting when there is a slump. It operates to slow up wage movements and to forestall chaos in the labor market.

To small employers, multi-employer bargaining gives strength and protection against unreasonable union demands. Far from tending to eliminate small business, Clark Kerr found that the extensive use of multi-employer bargaining of the administrative type in the San Francisco area gave the small employers a more effective voice in the determination of labor conditions. While no one has made a study of the subject, it is my belief that very generally the employers' associations which carry on collective bargaining are not controlled by their largest members, although this may be the case in coal mining. Employers in entering into multi-employer bargaining surrender some of their freedom to act as they see fit, but in doing so may attain more real freedom.

All these advantages of multi-employer bargaining are probably largely nonexistent in industries where, and at times when, there is little price competition. They also are of only slight, if any, importance to the very large and dominant corporations. These can eliminate wage competition and labor stealing to a very large extent by their own action, without combining with any other employers. And multi-employer bargaining always carries with it the price of losing some individual freedom of action and the possibility of being committed to some course which the particular corporation does not approve. For many employers,

these theoretical disadvantages, however, are more than outweighed by the practical advantages they derive from multi-employer bargaining.

Critics of industry-wide bargaining (in the loose usage of this term) are mainly concerned not with the effects upon employers but with alleged dangers to the public. They picture industry-wide collective bargaining as amounting to monopoly and as leading inevitably to higher prices and exploitation of the consumers. Considering only the actual experience to date, little evidence has appeared of such a result. Clark Kerr very positively reached the conclusion that prices have not been increased through multi-employer bargaining on the Pacific Coast,[3] and that was also the conclusion in the Princeton study of *Wages under National and Regional Collective Bargaining*.[4] High prices have prevailed in the post-war period both in industries in which there is multi-employer bargaining and in which the bargaining is on a plant or company basis, and also in unorganized industries. But the claimed tendency of multi-employer bargaining to produce higher prices may develop when prices become more responsive to costs as supplies increase and purchasers become more price-conscious.

The interests of the public are much broader than the lowest possible consumer prices. The purpose of all economic activity is human welfare, and this is not measured alone by the monetary price of goods and services. A stable supply is no less important than the price. It should ever be remembered also

[3] Clark Kerr, *Monthly Labor Review*, Vol. LXIV, No. 4 (April, 1947).

[4] By Richard A. Lester and E. A. Robie (Industrial Relations Section, Princeton University, 1946); see also Chapter 8 in Lester and Shister, *Insights into Labor Issues.*

that the workers are part of the public and in a democracy are numbered among the citizens and rulers of the country. Clearly, low prices are not either desirable or feasible if they depend upon the exploitation of labor. In a progressive economy, such as our system of free enterprise, moreover, standards of living should ever be rising for the workers and all others in our society.

The fear that market-wide bargaining may result in collusive agreements between employers and unions for the exploitation of the public also often voiced by the critics may not be unreal, but evidence that it has occurred is confined to a very few instances. To cope with such collusive agreements, we have the Sherman Anti-Trust Act. While unions are exempt from prosecution under that act in most of their activities, it is well established that they are subject to prosecution if they combine with employers to rig prices. If the law is not now adequate to deal with collusive agreements of this character, it should be strengthened. But that is a problem of its own. To prohibit multi-employer bargaining because collusive agreements may result is like burning the barn to get rid of the rats.

Beyond fears of monopoly and high prices, multi-employer bargaining is objected to on the ground that it increases the hazard of strikes seriously endangering the entire economy. Clark Kerr came to this conclusion in his study of associational bargaining on the Pacific Coast.[5] While such bargaining has reduced the number of strikes and the total strike losses, it has resulted in larger strikes or, more commonly, in the threat of crippling strikes which, fortunately, were settled before there was a stoppage. There is some ground for attributing the same

result to the approximation to true industry-wide bargaining which has been developed in the coal and railroad industries. It is also true, however, that great strikes have occurred where there was no multi-employer bargaining. The most prolonged nation-wide railroad strikes this country has had occurred as far back as 1877 and 1894, long before there was even system-wide bargaining on the railroads. With the exception of the coal and maritime strikes, nearly all the great postwar strikes have occurred in industries in which there is but little associational bargaining. Crippling strikes, moreover, may occur when the strikes themselves are not large. An unauthorized strike of only a few hundred operators of the tugboats in New York harbor in the fall of 1945 brought that greatest of world ports to a standstill and the entire city dangerously near exhaustion of food supplies. Somewhat more than a thousand workers in the power plants of Pittsburgh belonging to an independent union and opposed by the bulk of the public utility employees, in 1946, paralyzed all industry in that area and compelled shutdowns in many steel-consuming plants far from Pittsburgh.

It is not unlikely that market-wide bargaining may increase the hazard of great crippling strikes. But even if this be true, it does not inevitably lead to the conclusion that such bargaining should be prohibited by law. I agree with the view held by a majority of Americans that strikes seriously threatening the health, safety, and welfare of the nation cannot be allowed to go on. At this time when we have again just narrowly escaped such a strike, it is wholesome, however, to remember that so far we have always got through these crises without really disastrous results. The provisions of the Taft-Hartley Act relating

[5] Kerr, *op. cit.*

to strikes producing great emergencies, which nearly everyone described as very weak, to date have been the provisions of that law which have operated most successfully. Whether they will continue to do so is uncertain, but it is very clear that the problem of strikes producing great emergencies is one distinct from that of multi-employer or even actual industry-wide bargaining. Whatever is done about industry-wide bargaining will not solve this problem. It should be recognized as a problem of its own and dealt with accordingly.

This morning the further fear was expressed that industry-wide and company-wide bargaining will inevitably lead to increased governmental interference in labor-management relations. That there has been a strong trend toward increased governmental intervention is very certain. Under the Taft-Hartley Act, the government is much more extensively in labor-management relations than ever before. But it is doubtful whether industry-wide, company-wide, and multi-employer collective bargaining is an important factor accounting for this trend. I believe that one of the main factors lies in the size which corporations and unions have attained. However the bargaining is carried on, the size which the bargainers have attained affects the public in such a way that increased intervention on part of the government is inevitable whenever the public feels dissatisfied or is alarmed about the way things are going.

The surest way to get more governmental restrictions is to add to the existing restrictions. The legal restriction of industry-wide bargaining is an additional governmental restriction. As Cyrus Ching has often said, "Restrictions breed restrictions." Prohibiting industry-wide bargaining of itself represents an exten-

sion of governmental authority in labor relations and is likely to be followed ere long by further restrictions. This is a major reason why it is unwise to legislate against industry-wide bargaining. There is no clear stopping point in governmental intervention. Every additional governmental restriction affords reasons for further restrictions; and restrictions upon labor and management in their dealing with each other will also lead to further public regulation of other aspects of our economic system, with a real danger that our economy of free enterprise will give way to an economy controlled by the government in every aspect.

Industry-wide collective bargaining needs to be appraised in the light of the alternatives which have developed in this country. It is unrealistic to discuss this subject as if the choice lay between industry-wide bargaining and bargaining in which the terms are negotiated locally in the light of the peculiar conditions prevailing in the particular plant. What we have had in most of the major industries of the country is not industry-wide bargaining but union-wide bargaining and national wage patterns.

During the war the United Steelworkers started the practice of making identical demands upon all employers with whom they had contracts, including many companies not engaged in steel manufacture or anything connected therewith. Since then, this union has negotiated with the U. S. Steel Corporation and thereafter has used the agreement reached in these negotiations as the pattern for all unionized plants. It has made some concessions, indeed, but generally has insisted that the employers sign on the dotted line. Much the same situation has developed in automobile, rubber, and other mass production industries. We have had a first, second, and now a third round of wage increases applied generally in many different industries, with but few modifications. Wage increases, if not wage rates, have been standardized, to a very great extent, not merely in one industry but nationally. The contracts have been entered into separately for each company but there often has been but little negotiation with the firms upon whom demands have been made to follow the national wage pattern and scant, if any, consideration of their peculiar problems.

Collective bargaining as thus carried on produces all of the evils which critics charge against industry-wide bargaining. It gives individual employers far less of a voice in determining the conditions of employment in their plants than they have as members of associations which bargain on a multi-employer basis.

The extremes of national-wage-pattern bargaining we have had in the postwar period may disappear as a more normal demand and supply situation develops. So long as we have strong unions, however, they will seek standardization of wages and other major conditions of employment in the product market in which they operate. Employers, likewise, are greatly influenced by what other employers are doing. Following the pattern set by the bellwether corporations seems almost as common as in the following of patterns established by other unions.[6] . . .

I do not take the position that multi-employer bargaining is feasible or desirable in all industries and at all times. Such a conclusion might be drawn from the reports made in 1938 by President Roosevelt's commission to study industrial relations in England and Sweden,[7] which included among other industrialists, the then President of the National Manufacturers' Association. It was the recommendation of this commission for greatly extended use of industry-wide bargaining which started the present controversy.

Whether this recommendation was sound or unsound, the present issue is not whether industry-wide bargaining should be encouraged or promoted by government but whether it should be restricted or even outlawed. To me, it seems that this issue has been given undue importance. Still more strongly I believe that much further study is needed before sound judgment can be passed upon the wisdom of the many different arrangements to which this term has been applied.

Legislation on the subject, at the present state of knowledge, would be most hazardous. I see no need for such a further extension of governmental interference and regulation in labor-management relations. Instead, I believe that the government should keep hands off and allow labor and management to engage in multi-employer collective bargaining, if so inclined. . . .

[6] The tendency to follow the wage patterns set by large corporations applies particularly to their supplies. At least since the war there has been a pronounced tendency for the small producers and suppliers to hold back in reaching agreements with their unions until the large corporations in the industry have set the pattern. Much uniformity also results from the fact that even when employers bargain individually they often have the same attorneys and advisers who do the bargaining for many other employers. It is not literally true, as Emil Rieve has said, that true individual bargaining by employers acting independently no longer exists, but there may well be almost as much joint action in collective bargaining by employers as on the part of the unions.

[7] United States Commission to Study Industrial Relations in Great Britain, *Report with Appendices* (Washington, U. S. Department of Labor); United States Commission to Study Industrial Relations in Sweden, *Report with Appendices* (Washington, U. S. Department of Labor, 1938).

THREE STATEMENTS BY INDUSTRY

Walter B. Weisenburger · NATIONAL ASSOCIATION
OF MANUFACTURERS

SOME union spokesmen go on the assumption that, if it is a good thing for the employees in a plant to organize to bargain collectively, it must be even better for workers in an entire industry to bargain collectively. Aside from the possibility of carrying a good thing too far, these people do not realize that industry-wide collective bargaining is entirely different from collective bargaining at the plant level. It is far more than merely extending collective bargaining to a larger unit. There is a change in the very nature of the resulting negotiations.

Industry-wide and Plant Level Bargaining Differ

I think of collective bargaining as a method of determining wages, hours and working conditions for a given group of employees by a process of discussion, consideration and negotiation, and administration of the resultant agreement. The process is carried on by an employer on one side of the bargaining table and a union on the other — a union which is the freely chosen representative of the employees. Some of the union representatives are usually workers in the plant.

Now what is industry-wide collective bargaining? That is a situation where the employer's side of the table is occupied not only by one employer, but by a representative of all of the employers in the whole industry. He cannot be thoroughly familiar with the conditions and circumstances of any one plant, since he is required to know something about all the plants in the industry. Instead of a specific knowledge of particular facts, he must have a general knowledge of average conditions.

And who represents the union in industry-wide negotiations? Not the local union representative who devotes his major attention to the working conditions, wages and hours in a specific plant or company. The union representative in industry-wide bargaining is a national (or international) union president whose interest is no one specific plant or company, but who presumably knows something about the whole industry, and is concerned primarily about the union's national (or international) interests and policies. National union interests are paramount even if some particular company is thrown out of business, and its employees lose their jobs.

Which type of collective bargaining is likely to be most successful in meeting the needs of employers and workers? More important still, which type of bargaining is likely to serve the consumers who, in the final analysis, pay the worker's wage and the manager's salary?

The Individual Worker, the Forgotten Man of Industry-wide Bargaining

Let's look at collective bargaining from the viewpoint of an employee. I am not thinking of a nameless clock-number in a theoretical average plant. I am think-

From "Why Management Is Opposed to Industry-wide Collective Bargaining," by Walter B. Weisenburger, Executive Vice-president, National Association of Manufacturers. *The Sign* (January, 1947). Reprinted by permission.

ing of John H. Brown, who has a wife and two kids at home, and works as a milling machine operator at the C. A. Whyte Mfg. Company. John Brown has some very specific problems. In the first place, he's wondering what are his chances of getting another wage increase. Moreover, he suspects that his foreman showed favoritism in giving someone else the gravy jobs. He'd like to know whether the C. A. Whyte Mfg. Co. is making a 50% profit, as he heard at the last union meeting. And he'd like to know just how much chance he stands of being made a group leader, and maybe a foreman.

In other words, John Brown's chief interest lies in his particular job, his foreman, his company. And he joined his union because he believes his union can help him about some of these problems.

But who's worried about John Brown when it comes to industry-wide bargaining? The bargaining is carried on by people whom John Brown doesn't know and may never have heard of. They're discussing industry-wide problems. They may be concerned about tariffs and foreign competition and nation-wide conditions. They never heard of John Brown and don't know what his problems are. They get involved in such things as regional differentials, uniform standards, long-range trends in the industry. That doesn't help John Brown one bit.

He reads in the newspapers about the negotiations. Sure, maybe he'll get a wage raise out of it. But is he going to have to go on strike again just because a couple of negotiators in Washington (or Pittsburgh, or New York) couldn't get together? He remembers the steel strike of 1945 when he and hundreds of others were told to "hit the bricks" even though there was no dispute with his employer. He knows that his local union officers understand his problems, but he is

rightly afraid that the international union president never heard of him. Brown knows that he and his local union officers can talk things over with C. A. Whyte, the President of the Company, and can usually reach an understanding; but he knows very little about this employer negotiator who represents the whole industry and he fears the worst. Why can't the local union and individual employer or plant manager settle their problems right at home instead of passing the buck to somebody a thousand miles away?

Industry-wide Bargaining Encourages Union Autocracy

In the long run industry-wide bargaining encourages more and more concentration of union power and authority in a few hands at the top and less and less real autonomy in the membership at the local level. The United Mine Workers offers a shining example of concentrated union power which flourishes under industry-wide bargaining.

There is also the possibility that a union will obtain a closed shop on a national basis. Should this happen, the hierarchy of officials in charge of that union acquires the power to determine whether any individual citizen shall have the right to earn a living in that industry in any part of the nation. Surely it would be tempting fate to take any step which would give any group such power over individuals.

The Employer Prefers to Deal Directly with the Local Union

And what about the employer? Some employers, it is true, have become so fed up with abuses of collective bargaining that they've been quite willing to let someone else handle this problem child. But in general, once employers are convinced that their employees voluntarily elect to bargain collectively, the average employer undertakes his collective bargaining responsibilities as an integral part of his job as an employer, and tries to make it work. But he is confused and mystified by union insistence on industry-wide bargaining. Except as a competitor, he is not interested in the rest of the industry of which his company is a part. He is ready and willing to bargain collectively with his employees and their representatives. He does not understand why he should become involved in negotiations with other companies having entirely different problems. Nor does he understand why he should be faced with a strike when there is no dispute between him and his employees.

Industry-wide Bargaining Threatens the Public Welfare

But it is from a viewpoint of the public that industry-wide bargaining looks most suspicious. Here are some points that lead me to the definite conclusion that industry-wide bargaining is a threat to the public welfare.

1. Practical experience shows that the better a labor agreement meets the needs and problems of a particular group of employees and a particular management, the better it promotes stable and satisfactory labor relations. The old adage about fitting square pegs into square holes and round pegs into round holes holds true in labor relations as in other human activities. If it does not meet the needs of employees and employers at the local level, collective bargaining will not result in industrial peace. And industrial peace is what the people of this country demand.

2. If collective bargaining agreements are not negotiated at the plant level, the people in the plants cannot fully understand them. They will have difficulty in administering negotiated agreements. A badly worded agreement that is fully understood is better than a model agreement which labor and management at the plant level cannot understand. Lack of understanding can only lead to industrial strife.

3. If labor and management at the plant level have negotiated an agreement, they will both do their very best to make it work. But if they have an agreement thrust upon them by national negotiators from Washington or New York, their natural reaction will be to find fault with it and declare that somebody ought to have his head examined. There will be little inducement to try to make it work.

4. The public has a tremendous stake in the maintenance of effective competition. Industry-wide bargaining tends to stifle competition in two ways: (1) Collective bargaining on an industry-wide basis may lead to other activities on an industry-wide basis equally inconsistent with free competition; (2) To the extent that industry-wide bargaining results in uniform wages, it drives marginal companies out of business, thereby throwing workers out of jobs.

5. If we endorse collective bargaining, we must accept the right of the employees to strike if good faith bargaining does not give them the kind of agreement which they believe they should have. A strike in a plant is unfortunate, but may be justified as the price we must pay for free collective bargaining in a free economy. But a strike which closes down an entire industry is intolerable, and is bound to bring government intervention. Government intervention prevents free collective bargaining, and may lead to increasing government control of industry and of labor.

Let those who endorse industry-wide collective bargaining consider whether the doubtful advantages and conveniences of industry-wide negotiations are worth the loss of free industry and free labor unions.

6. Aside from industry-wide strikes, bargaining on an industry-wide basis tends to become less and less an economic problem, and assumes a more and more political complexion. The farther from the plant level, the more likely the negotiations are to be based on matters of principle and strategy. Negotiations are much more likely to revolve about ideology rather than about the needs of John H. Brown, the milling machine operator at the C. A. Whyte Mfg. Co. Do we want to settle our collective bargaining problems by political means? I think not. Moreover, the resulting agreement may actually put the C. A. Whyte Mfg. Co. out of business, since the agreement is based on conditions of the industry rather than those of one company. It is little solace to John H. Brown, as he is laid off, to know that the new agreement is excellent for the industry.

7. Opinion polls have shown that the public is concerned about the excessive powers of national union leaders. That excessive power is strengthened by industry-wide collective bargaining. It puts tremendous power in the hands of a very few. That power is subject to abuse. It has led two labor leaders to defy the government of the United States itself. The examples of John L. Lewis and James Caesar Petrillo may well make the staunchest friends of labor hesitate to encourage the kind of bargaining upon which these men have waxed powerful and arrogant.

8. Industry-wide bargaining may lead to ever greater concentration of industry in fewer hands. Agreement to uniform terms may help the larger, more efficient units in an industry to freeze out the small or less efficient manufacturers. Any practice which tends to encourage ever greater concentration and to discourage newcomers should certainly be avoided.

9. Industry-wide bargaining offers an extremely fertile field for those whose primary interest lies, not in advancing the people's standards of living, but in overthrowing our system of competitive enterprise and political freedom. It offers opportunities for wide-spread critical strikes, dictatorial control, and government intervention. Plant level collective bargaining gets at the grass roots problems where they can best be handled; industry-wide collective bargaining leads to the rarefied atmosphere of ideological clashes.

10. The American competitive enterprise system has been marked by diversity, freedom, flexibility and opportunity for individual initiative. That is why it has been able to produce the world's highest standard of living, and goods and services in great abundance. Freedom to experiment, to try the unorthodox, to seek better ways of production is vital to the health of competitive enterprise. Industry-wide bargaining introduces rigidities and encourages deadening uniformity.

Lessons of other countries, with similar territories and more homogenous working populations, are not applicable to the United States. Our laws, our traditions, our concepts of what is right — all differ. Some countries have no laws against monopolies. We do. And for the same reasons that we wholeheartedly oppose monopolies, we should especially oppose industry-wide bargaining.

It is true that there are cases of "industry-wide" bargaining which have worked very well over a limited period of time and in a limited geographic area. These examples do not prove the soundness of a fundamentally dangerous practice any more than does a specific case of a benevolent dictatorship prove that dictatorships are sound.

There are some union spokesmen who characterize our opposition to industry-wide bargaining as an effort to "divide and conquer." I want to make it clear that I demand no more "division" on the labor side than now exists on the management side. Let the national unions represent their members in the way the NAM, for example, represents its members. We do not and will not bargain collectively for our members. We do not issue instructions for them to follow. We interpret the views of industry to the public and to the government; and we seek to raise management's sights to ever higher levels of achievement and ever higher standards of performance.

But we do not bargain for our members. We do not formulate any common plan of action. And we certainly do not seek to undermine or "fight" labor unions. That is a time honored myth assiduously cultivated by the more vocal labor spokesmen when they need a convenient scapegoat.

A spokesman for the C.I.O. has said that he is looking forward to the day when the Presidents of the C.I.O. and A.F.L. can sit down and bargain collectively with appropriate representatives of industry for all the workers of the United States. With all the vehemence at my command, I say that I hope that that day never comes. For when it does, free collective bargaining and free competitive enterprise will both be dead.

Charles S. Craigmile · ILLINOIS MANUFACTURERS' ASSOCIATION

MR. CRAIGMILE. I am Charles S. Craigmile. I am executive vice president of the Belden Manufacturing Co. We manufacture insulated copper wire, with a plant in Chicago, Ill., and one in Richmond, Ind. We have a total of about 1,600 people in those two plants.

I am here today representing the Illinois Manufacturers' Association, of approximately 4,300 members, of the State of Illinois, as the chairman of their industrial relations committee.

The Illinois Manufacturers' Association has repeatedly pointed out that the Wagner Act embraces a mandate from Congress to unionize American industry; that the National Labor Relations Board, pursuant to such mandate and acting as prosecutor, judge, and jury, has carried on a vigorous campaign to extend and to perpetuate the domination of American industry by union labor leaders; that the so-called majority rule principle in said act strips the worker of individual freedom and constitutes an irresistible invitation to labor leaders to promote strife and unrest in industry with the object of securing sole bargaining rights; that the

From Hearings on S. 55, and S. J. Res. 22, United States Senate, Committee on Labor and Public Welfare, 80th Congress, 1st Session, part 1, February, 1947, pp. 515–524.

National Labor Relations Board has established a collection of rulings and regulations which constitute a policy of Government control over labor relations which must be eliminated if industry is to be freed from the monopolistic power of labor-union leaders; that these characteristics are inherent in and represent the fundamental philosophy of the act, and that such characteristics cannot be eliminated by amendment or revision, and that, accordingly, repeal of the Wagner Act is essential if industrial peace and stability in employment relations are to be accomplished.

The Congress is accordingly, I respectfully submit, clearly confronted with the necessity of nurturing and undertaking to control a menacing national juggernaut, or of withdrawing the special congressional grants of power and privilege by which this menacing national juggernaut was built and is constantly being extended.

I will get right down to the crux of the matter:

First, the monopolistic power of the labor-union leaders already threatens daily the stability of the Nation. Tens of millions of employees, inside and outside the labor unions, thousands of employers, big and little, and the public generally, live from day to day in abject fear of a handful of labor-union leaders. And the power of these men is increasing day by day. This is the national juggernaut I refer to.

Second, this monopolistic power, this juggernaut, is built upon and is constantly maintained and extended by special congressional grant of power and privilege which for some unaccountable reason most people do not recognize or understand.

I refer to the grant by Congress of what is called majority rule under the Wagner Act.

The Wagner Act makes the following special grant of power and privilege to labor unions:

Sec. 9 (a). Representatives designated . . . by the majority of the employees in a unit . . . shall be the exclusive representative of all the employees in such unit . . . in respect to rates of pay, wages, hours of employment, or other conditions of employment . . .

Under this special grant of power by Congress, the labor union that once secures designation by a majority of the employees in a craft unit, a plant unit, or an industry-wide unit secures and holds this amazingly great and un-American control over all the employees in that unit:

1. That labor union completely and exclusively supplants every employee in that unit concerning the determination of the wages he shall work for, the hours he shall work, and the conditions of his employment.

2. That labor union completely and exclusively supplants every employee in that unit concerning the settlement of any grievance he may have in connection with his employment or his work.

3. That labor union completely and exclusively supplants every employee in that unit concerning the determination of whether he shall, as a condition of holding his job, join the union, support the union financially, and support the policies and practices of the union.

Under section 9 (a) of the Wagner Act, the "majority union" has, under this majority rule provision, the exclusive authority to determine upon, to bargain for, and to agree to, all the terms of the contract under which every employee in the unit, whether he is and has been for or against being represented by that union, must work and live — all the terms of the contract concerning his wages, his hours of work, his conditions of employment, and whether and to what extent he will be subject to any variety of the closed shop and check-off.

Please keep this in mind at all times: Unbelievable as it should be, the individual or the group in the minority, whether the minority consists of 1 workman or 20,000 workmen, is thus forced by act of Congress to accept and be supplanted by a labor union that he does not want, in all matters that concern his wages, his hours of work, his conditions of employment, and, whether he will be required to join, to contribute to, and to support the policies and activities of that labor union.

If this is not slavery by act of Congress, what would you call it? . . .

The Illinois Manufacturers' Association does not seek any legislation that would grant anyone any special privilege. We seek liberty and freedom for the individual. We seek equality before the law for everyone.

The Illinois Manufacturers' Association will support legislation that will protect the rights of everyone alike to freedom, liberty, and equality before the law.

We propose:

1. Repeal the Wagner Act and its grant of special power and privilege of majority rule under the Wagner Act.

2. Enact, if you think it advisable, legislation which embodies the following principles:

(a) Freedom of every employee at all times to deal with his employer, as an individual or through collective bargaining through a labor union of his choice, as he wishes.

(b) Freedom of every employee at all times to work or to refrain from work without molestation, as he wishes.

(c) Equality under the law at all times for the individual, whether he is in the majority, in the minority, or whether he stands alone.

*   *   *

SENATOR MORSE. . . . Do you think that the repeal of the Wagner Act and the adoption of a program which you recommend to the committee would be very helpful to those forces in the country that want to aid an open-shop drive?

MR. CRAIGMILE. I should answer "yes" to that question, Senator, because I believe that naturally without the compulsion you would have more open-shop conditions in the country, and, therefore, anybody that advocates, as many people do, an open shop would be aided in that program.

SENATOR MORSE. You are an advocate of the open shop?

MR. CRAIGMILE. I am.

Tyre Taylor · SOUTHERN STATES INDUSTRIAL COUNCIL

MR. TAYLOR. My name is Tyre Taylor. I appear here on behalf of the Southern States Industrial Council as their general counsel. The Southern States is an organization of some 4,000 individual industries and concerns distributed through the 16 Southern States. . . .

Coal mining is one of the South's major industries and its efficient operation is enormously important, not only to the industry itself but all consumers of its products. Most of our members are commercial or industrial users of coal, and I voice their feeling when I commend this committee for its decision to conduct these hearings. The refusal of the committee to ignore or minimize the crisis which union monopolies have created in this country is a bright spot in an otherwise extremely dark and disturbing picture. . . .

I should like first to discuss the nature of the labor monopoly which exists in coal, though a similar situation prevails in rail transportation and, to a lesser degree, in steel and other basic industries.

The first thing to be said about this monopoly is that it is absolute. For all practical purposes, the UMW exercises total control over coal production in this country. I think we can go even further and say that, in this particular situation, the monopoly is personal. A single individual — Mr. John L. Lewis — has it in his power to suspend production entirely — as he has done in the numerous industry-wide strikes of recent years. Or he can systematically curtail production — while at the same time successfully stalling against collective bargaining — as he is now doing through the imposition of the 3-day week.

John D. Rockefeller, Sr., never exercised one-tenth of the control over oil that John L. Lewis now exercises over coal. Indeed, it may be seriously questioned whether, under our Constitution, Congress itself has such authority in peacetime.

A second characteristic of this monopoly in coal, rail transportation, and certain other industries is that it directly affects the national welfare. Not only is every prolonged strike in coal or rail transportation a "national emergency" strike which endangers the health and safety of vast numbers of our people, but union restrictive and monopolistic practices applied to these basic industries weaken the entire economy and constitute a most serious threat to our free competitive system. I shall go into this latter point further when I discuss the manner in which this power is being exercised and its effects upon the various segments of the economy.

A third characteristic of this monopoly is that, at least up to the present, it is strictly a union monopoly. It is not participated in by management. On the contrary — and except for the periods when the NRA code was in effect and the Guffey Coal Act was in force — the coal industry as such has been intensively competitive. Needless to say, if it should ever come about that the operators as a group connive with the union to restrict production and control prices, we would have the same type of labor-management charter which Italy had under fascism and which Germany had and Britain has under national socialism. I have read with the greatest concern the news reports to the effect that consideration is

From Hearings on Economic Power of Labor Organizations, U. S. Senate Committee on Banking and Currency, 81st Congress, 1st Session, part 1, pp. 176–189.

being given to the setting up of a czar in the bituminous-coal industry. If the purpose or effect of any such move is to make the operators parties to the existing union monopoly, it would, in our opinion, be illegal under existing law.

At this point, it should be observed that in its dealings with these union monopolies, management has very often had to contend with an alliance between the Federal Government and the union in which Federal agencies and officials have assisted and espoused the union's cause. For at least the last 6 years — and continuing up until the present time — the executive branch has pursued this partisan policy, and in certain industries such as coal it has resulted in making free collective bargaining unworkable for management and unprofitable for unions. The history of the Government's seizures of bituminous mines and the concessions won by the UMW as a result explains as well as anything the reason for the perpetual labor crisis in coal. True collective bargaining in the industry is dead and recurring crises will plague the Nation until it is restored.

A fourth characteristic of the monopoly and the final one which I shall discuss is its assumption of the basic managerial function of determining the manner and extent to which the owners shall utilize their properties. As the New York Times commented editorially on July 27:

Management not only has the right to operate on the schedule which will result in the most efficient, and therefore the lowest cost production; it has a duty to the public to insist upon recognition of that right.

Of course, from the standpoint of management, the situation presently existing in coal is intolerable and if continued will destroy the value of the properties and make impossible their continued effi-cient operation for the benefit of all the people.

How the power is exercised: So far we have noted that the UMW and other industry-wide unions have unrestrained monopoly control over absolutely essential commodities and services. A very pertinent question raised by your committee is how this power is exercised. Of course paralyzing industry-wide strikes and the threat of such strikes are the weapons which the unions use so effectively to bludgeon management and the public, but how does it come about that John L. Lewis, for example, is able to command some 400,000 individual workers as a general commands an army? What is the explanation of this astonishing discipline?

Of course Mr. Lewis is in a position to exercise practically absolute control over the lives and livelihoods of the individual workers. Taft-Hartley and the various State anti-closed-shop laws to the contrary notwithstanding, the UMW operates as one of the tightest closed shops in the world. And every increase in the special union levied tax for the welfare fund serves to strengthen the union's economic hold over the workers and therefore over the entire industry. The union has the exclusive right, protected by law, to the exclusion of the worker himself, to negotiate the wages, hours of work, retirement benefits, and other terms and conditions of employment. . . .

The UMW is not only a complete monopoly. From the standpoint of its members, it is an immensely successful monopoly. I never heard of the stockholders of a business monopoly complaining of the management so long as dividends were high and constantly increasing. But neither have I ever heard it suggested that stockholder enthusiasm in such situations should constitute a defense to an indictment for violation of the antitrust laws.

Effects upon the economy: The third aspect of this problem which, Mr. Chairman, you have suggested that witnesses discuss is the effect of the exercise of this monopolistic power on the various segments of our economy. I should like to do this now and with particular reference to the South and to southern industry.

The first and most immediate effect is, of course, to raise the price of coal to all consumers and to dislocate the system of distribution and supply. The 3-day week — or strike-every-Thursday — edict results in a 40-percent reduction in working time, and the experience up to now indicates that this means a decrease in production of at least 50 percent. This means that fixed costs must be borne by half the customary production. You have heard various tentative estimates as to the amount of this increase per ton and they have ranged from 10 cents for the most efficient, lowest cost operations to $1 per ton for the marginal mines. These added costs must be and are already being partially reflected in price increases. If we strike an average of, say, 40 cents, it is possible for the industrial or home consumer to estimate a part of the direct cost to him of this union-imposed restraint upon production.

This, of course, is the immediate, direct increase in costs and prices at the mines. It does not take into account any pyramiding of these increases in subsequent stages of distribution and manufacture, or any possible reduction in prevailing coal prices if the economic law of supply and demand were permitted to operate.

Nor does it take into account the immediate and direct effect of this restraint on production upon industries — such as some of the railroads — whose earnings depend upon the production and distribution of coal. . . .

What the UMW monopoly has done in coal, other industry-wide labor monopolies have the power to do in steel, rail transportation, ocean shipping, the operation of our public utilities, the manufacture of automobiles, farm machinery, and so on. If the restraint of production established by Lewis in coal should be extended to steel and other basic industries, the country would quickly face the kind of want and misery now being endured by the people of Britain, where precisely such restrictive practices are not only permitted but encouraged by the Socialist government. And perhaps this offers a clue to the strange absence of leftist criticism of Mr. Lewis. Is not his restrictionist policy the best argument that could possibly be advanced for the nationalization of the coal industry? And is this not precisely what our totalitarian "liberals" want?

How we got where we are: There is a tendency to blame the union bosses for most of the evils arising from labor monopolies. In particular, Mr. Lewis has been the target of a great deal of criticism, especially from the politicians.

This, I submit, is at least somewhat lacking in both fairness and candor. Mr. Lewis did not enact the provision of the Clayton Act which exempts labor unions from the antitrust laws. He did not enact the N. I. R. A., or the Norris-LaGuardia Act, or the National Labor Relations Act. Congress enacted all these laws. Nor did Mr. Lewis decide the Hutcheson and Allen Bradley cases, whereby the exemption of the unions from the antitrust laws was judicially confirmed and established. The Supreme Court did that.

In other words, it has been the public policy of the United States for many years now to build up the UMW and other unions into the great monopolies they have become. Mr. Lewis is only exercising the powers which Congress gave him. The Government itself — the Congress, the Executive, and the Supreme Court — established the policy. They established the rule that what is antisocial and wrong and hence illegal — if done by businessmen — is not wrong or antisocial if done by a union or combination of unions. They established the double standard under which the coal operators would go to jail if they did what Mr. Lewis does with impunity. They set up labor unions as a class apart from the general population, a specially favored class for which there was not to be equal justice under law, but special privilege. Under this policy, the unions even became and remain to this day political adjuncts of the Government itself. I doubt whether Mr. Lewis saw anything incongruous in his recent insistence on the right of veto over a Presidential appointment.

Was it not required that a Vice Presidential nomination — as it turned out, one of the most fateful in history — be "cleared with Sidney?" And do we not hear all recordings of our National Anthem "by the courtesy of James C. Petrillo?" And is not another of these labor monopolists currently conducting a blockade of the Hawaiian Islands, which are supposed to be a Territory and under the protection of the United States?

While it is stated that it is not the function of this committee to recommend corrective legislation directly to the Senate, I should nevertheless like to summarize the two suggestions we made this time last year to the Joint Committee on Labor-Management Relations. They are:

1. Amend the Labor-Management Relations Act to include the railroads, and require that bargaining units in the coal, steel-producing, and rail-transportation industries be on a company-wide basis, with all other bargaining units restricted to a metropolitan district, county, or a company-wide basis.

2. Amend the Clayton Act and the Norris-LaGuardia Act (a) to make unlawful any combination, contract, conspiracy, or concerted plan of action between any person or corporation represented in different bargaining units, whose operation is required to be autonomous under point No. 1 above, where the object of such activity is to formulate a policy with regard to the terms or conditions of collective-bargaining agreements, or to agree on a time or plan for carrying out a strike, lock-out, slow-down, or other interference with trade or production; and (b) to make it unlawful for any labor organization or its agents to make any contract or to engage in any combination or conspiracy in restraining of trade if one of the purposes of such contract, combination, or conspiracy is to fix prices, allocate consumers, or restrict production, distribution, or competition.

What you are dealing with, Mr. Chairman, in this hearing is nothing less than the basic dilemma of our age. Everywhere the forces of freedom are in full retreat before the most ghastly reaction of modern times, a reaction which, in the main, is sparked by greed and lust for power. In Britain, for example, the rapacious, deluded people have embarked upon a socialistic program of loot and confiscation, but are now in the process of finding out -- perhaps too late — that this course leads only to total regimentation, universal poverty, and individual and national degradation and loss of self-respect.

Here you are dealing with a manifestation of the same insane greed and lust for power. In order to have their way, a few ruthless union bosses are quite willing not only to ruin their own industries by pricing their products out of the market, but to wreck the free-enterprise system itself.

I do not know why Congress has not acted to correct this condition long before now. All of us know in our hearts that the Government-imposed double standard for management and unions is utterly immoral and wrong; and that the concept of equal justice under law is no more than a mockery unless it requires that a crime be deemed a crime, no matter by whom committed.

We also know that these labor monopolies exact a toll from every last one of us; that, but for the existence of this enormous concentration of power in the hands of a few rapacious unioneers, the scale of living of the vast majority of the people would be materially higher than

it now is; and that, as is always the case with monopoly, whether exercised by Government, business, or a labor union, its paralyzing effects are cumulative.

I know it has been widely supposed that the New Deal–Fair Deal policy of fostering, pampering, favoring, and cringing before these monstrous Frankensteins is smart politics. Not being an expert in this highly complicated realm of human endeavor, I would not know.

I will, however, in conclusion venture an assertion which I doubt will be challenged by any member of this committee. It is that, in addition to all his other offenses against the general welfare which should impel Congress to trim him down to size, John L. Lewis has become an insufferable bore. His acting is ham, his utterances corny, his posturing pompous and silly. From this, too, a lot of long-suffering citizens would welcome deliverance.

FOUR STATEMENTS BY LABOR

William Green · AMERICAN FEDERATION OF LABOR

THE proposal that all contracts between employers and employees be confined to a local labor market strikes at the heart of the free collective-bargaining process. It would destroy long-established and mature collective-bargaining relations in many key areas of industry. Industrial peace was unbroken over a period of many years in many such areas because the scope of agreement between labor and management has been extended to cover more than

one plant and more than one employer. Labor-management relations did not break down and no work stoppages occurred at the most critical stage of industrial conflict in the difficult transition from war to peace since VJ-day where effective machinery for direct and voluntary settlement of differences was developed through area-wide, association-wide, and industry-wide agreements. That is precisely the area the proposed legislation would invade and that is the

From Hearings on S. 55 and S. J. Res. 22, Committee on Labor and Public Welfare, United States Senate, 80th Congress, 1st Session, part 2, February 1947, pp. 1032–1035.

procedure this legislation would outlaw.

In the glass bottle manufacturing industry, in the pottery and chinaware-manufacturing industry, in the stove manufacturing industry, in dress manufacturing, in pulp and paper manufacturing, and many others, there have been no strikes or lock-outs, no interruptions in production, and no cause for Government intervention during the crucial 20 months since the end of the war. In all these instances, area-wide, industry-wide, and association-wide A. F. of L. agreements proved to be the most effective instruments of labor peace. They have withstood the supreme test of inflationary pressures, dislocation, and discord of the most trying reconversion period. Yet these tested tools of industrial harmony and accord would be thrown on the scrap heap by the proposed legislation in the name of promoting industrial peace.

Government-dictated Formulas Were the Real Source of Evil

The attack against industry-wide bargaining is aimed at conditions remote from free collective bargaining. It is directed at the evil which has already been eradicated by the termination of war-time controls over wages. Under the war-time wage-stabilization program, continued in peace-time until recently, wage terms and other conditions agreed to by a few firms dominating an industry were imposed upon other firms in the industry. In such instances, the bargaining process was confined to a few giant aggregates in the industry. The smaller firms were compelled to sign up without even a pretense at negotiations. The "formula" was a part of a Government directive. Neither the employer nor the union had much choice; they acted under orders. In all such instances there was no collective bargaining. Industry-wide

standards so imposed were not the subject of real negotiation or real agreement.

None of these instances, therefore, were instances of industry-wide collective bargaining. The very nature of the procedure used was repugnant to the voluntary process of free collective bargaining. Such procedure was often regarded as an evil by both employers and unions. That evil has been ended with the end of Government controls on wages and the end of the war-time regulation over labor disputes. The real target of the proponents of this legislation is now gone. The high-explosive charge they have readied against that target must not be belatedly misdirected and allowed to destroy the very roots of industrial peace.

Long-established Agreements Must Not Be Destroyed by Law

Proposed legislation would strike at the very areas where harmonious and peaceful relations have been achieved after years of building up mutual confidence and good will between labor and management.

The outstanding feature of collective bargaining relations in the areas of industry where peaceful relations have been firmly established is that the scope of collective bargaining agreement is determined by the parties themselves in order better to fit the agreement to the conditions prevailing in each particular situation. As our industry and trade represent a widely varying pattern, so the coverage of collective-bargaining agreements shows wide variation.

The agreement may cover an individual employer or a single plant of that employer or a single class of workers or a single craft. Or it may cover, as is often the case, a dozen or a score of plants of the same employer, located in every part of the United States, or it may be an association-wide agreement which is the result of a joint negotiation by a number of employers who have chosen to participate in the negotiation jointly. The effective coverage of a union agreement cannot be arbitrarily determined by one party to negotiations. The scope of the agreement and of the procedures and relationships it establishes can only be the result of a mutual accord reached by the representatives of the employers and the employees. It cannot be defined or enforced by law.

Industry-wide Bargaining Is the Result of Growth

The more extensive coverage of collective-bargaining agreements is the result of growth in collective-bargaining relations and is characteristic of their maturity. The variable and complex structure of bargaining units as it exists today must be viewed in the historical perspective of its development.

Sixty-six years ago, when the American Federation of Labor was formed, industry in general confined its production to local plants and was to a much greater extent producing for local, rather than national markets. Trade and services were almost entirely in the hands of local business enterprises. Consider for example that 90 per cent of meat slaughter was then done by the farmer under a tree. In contrast, well over 90 per cent of meat slaughter today is a part of a nation-wide industrial operation in the hands of large nation-wide industrial aggregates. Most flour milling was then done by local millers, located on or near the farms, not national industrial operations that we know today. There were no chain-store groceries and no coast-to-coast chain outlets for hats, dresses, and a multitude of other commodities. Large-scale mass production and mass distribu-

tion in a national market was then still in its infancy. Today it dominates the industrial scene.

These changing conditions have changed substantially the scope and nature of collective-bargaining relations. The growth of large-scale business enterprise and the increased organization of employees into trade unions called for the wider scope of coverage of union agreements and for more uniform treatment of labor standards negotiated through these agreements.

The record shows that the widening of the scope of collective bargaining beyond a single plant or a single employer has been often sought by employers themselves. Large corporations have frequently found it desirable to establish uniformity in wages, hours and working conditions among their several plants. In many instances a trade association has entered the collective-bargaining relations and has become the spokesman for its several member companies. At the same time, many unions have found that in areas where other production costs had been equalized, cutthroat competition was carried on at the expense of wage standards. Such wage competition, undermining the standards attained, with disastrous consequences to the community, could best be prevented through equalization of wage rates under association-wide agreements.

Industry-wide Agreements Provide Machinery for Peaceful Settlement of Disputes

In other situations the sole objective of both the employers and the unions was to establish an orderly voluntary procedure for negotiations, handling of grievances and the settlement of disputes. There are a number of nation-wide agreements which cover such procedures, designed to safeguard peaceful relations in the industry. Such agreements leave wage negotiations to individual plants or establishments but provide a national or association-wide machinery for the settlement of disputes. Among the many examples of this type of agreement is one established between the American Federation of Grain Processors and the General Mills Corp. The nation-wide collective agreement covers all of the corporation's plants but leaves wage determination to local bargaining. Many other affiliates of the A. F. of L. have negotiated over a period of years nation-wide or association-wide or industry-wide agreements with employers in their respective industry or occupation. . . .

Many of the collective-bargaining contracts negotiated by more than one employer have been characterized by improvements in working standards together with greater stability and efficiency for the industry. In most cases, this has been accomplished without any work stoppages. In the pressed and blown glassware industry, for example, there has been no major strike since the start of industry-wide bargaining between the American Flint Glass Workers Union and the National Association of Manufacturers of Pressed and Blown Glassware in 1888. Here is a record of 60 years of uninterrupted industrial peace achieved through industry-wide collective bargaining. . . .

Among the many instances of association-wide bargaining agreements, a few additional examples deserve special mention. The United Association of Journeymen Plumbers and Steamfitters of the United States and Canada, A. F. of L., maintains an agreement with the National Automatic Sprinkler Association in the sprinkler fitting industry. In the wallpaper manufacturing industry the United

Wallpaper Craftsmen and Workers of North America, A. F. of L., maintains an agreement with the Wallpaper Institute. In the paper mill wire cloth manufacturing industry an association-wide agreement is maintained by the American Wire Weavers' Protective Association. In the elevator manufacturing and installation industry a long-established association-wide agreement is in effect between the International Union of Elevator Constructors, A. F. of L., and the National Elevator Manufacturing Industry, Inc.

In the case of the retail meat trade, the Amalgamated Meat Cutters and Butcher Workmen of America have maintained a national agreement with the National Association of Retail Meat Dealers. While this agreement serves as a basis for the promotion of positive policies of union-management cooperation, it does not cover wages or employment conditions which are negotiated locally. In the canning industry on the west coast, collective bargaining is conducted by the International Brotherhood of Teamsters, A. F. of L., on an association basis with employers in the area. The shipbuilding and boatbuilding industry on the west coast is covered by a master agreement negotiated by the metal trades department of the A. F. of L. on behalf of its constituent unions. Regional or area-wide agreements with whole associations of employers have been maintained by A. F. of L. affiliates in women's clothing, men's hats, and millinery industries, as well as in a number of other industries and trades.

According to a study recently completed by the Bureau of Labor Statistics of the United States Department of Labor:

More than 4 million workers are covered by agreements negotiated with associations and groups of employers. Most of the agreements are products of peaceful employer-union relations of several years' and some of several decades' duration.

Industry and regional bargaining has been successful in achieving its basic objectives, greater standardization of wages and employment conditions. This has meant greater stability for the industry, generally higher wages and at the same time fewer bankruptcies and a higher proportion of the firms returning a fair profit. . . .

Through the free collective-bargaining process, unions and employers mutually determine the form of their collective agreements and fit it to the most effective way of solving the problems both confront. In many cases over the past 50 years, the scope of these agreements has been enlarged in response to the growth of large-scale enterprises and the increasing interdependence of related business enterprises. Statutory limitation of labor agreements to a single locality is a direct attack upon the process of free collective bargaining. Any such attempt to confine collective bargaining to a specific area will turn back the clock of industrial progress.

Philip Murray · CONGRESS OF INDUSTRIAL ORGANIZATIONS

WE in the labor movement have had more than our share of the experience of being subject to abuse and attack. As organizations operating in a field of many hostilities and conflicting interests, we expect and assume that many of those whose economic interests are opposed to those of our members will harbor an antipathy toward us and give voice to their views. . . .

The campaign of recent months seeking passage of measures which follow this long line of past proposals differs from those of prior years primarily in its intensity, its scope, and its vigor. By speech, by press, by radio, by congressional proposal, by any and all of a numberless variety of devices, this Nation has been blanketed with a steady barrage of propaganda, of persuasion, of pressure, of innuendo — all seeking to build up a single direction and line of thought — that the major ills of our Nation are attributable to one group, to one class — labor, and that our salvation lies in subjecting this culprit to limitations, to curbs, to restrictions, all in the public interest. . . .

Is labor the culprit? Are we in a situation where there is the slightest validity to this mad campaign to chastise American working men and women? What are our current ills and where are their causes? What are our current difficulties and whose are the responsibilities? What has been labor's role in our economy? Has it been a force for good or for evil? What is the role which labor is playing today? Is its program constructive and helpful or otherwise? . . .

Before the war ended I said, "To correct the drift toward totalitarianism in this country, the role of all those groups seeking to maintain full employment and

From Hearings on S. 55 and S. J. Res. 22, Committee on Labor and Public Welfare, Labor Relations Program. United States Senate, 80th Congress, 1st Session, part 2, February 1947, pp. 1121–1125, 1139–1141.

democracy in industry and Government must be strengthened. The groups among big business who agree with us as to the need to resist this drift . . . should welcome and promote the joint participation of all like-minded groups in the program for transformation of our economy from war to peace, and the maintenance of full employment in the transition period. . . ."

The time is very late but it is not too late. We can achieve an expanding peacetime economy of full production and full employment by measures of cooperation between industry, labor, and agriculture which run directly counter to the present drift. But Congress must make clear to the people of this country that it will not tolerate the efforts of monopoly to defeat the possibility of achieving such cooperation. We cannot move far down the road of punitive legislation against labor inspired by monopoly industry and invoked by the legislative arm of government without disastrous consequences. . . .

Have you gentlemen considered the implications of the fact that 250 large corporations control two-thirds of the usable manufacturing facilities of our entire country? Have you considered the implications of the fact that by reliable calculation more than 100 of the largest corporations in our Nation are controlled by 8 groups of banking interests?

In the steel industry, the 10 largest corporations hold more than three-fourths of the ingot production capacity; 3 banking houses control 8 of those 10 producers.

As reported to the Temporary National Economic Committee by the Securities and Exchange Commission, approximately eight-thousandths of 1 per cent of the population own one-fourth of all the corporate stock in the country and approximately six-hundredths of 1 per

cent of the population own one-half of all the corporate stock in the country.

Among the largest 200 nonfinancial corporations, the top 1 percent of the book shareholders accounted for 60 per cent of the common-stock shares outstanding.

As of 1935, among the 200 largest nonfinancial corporations and the 50 largest financial corporations a group of some 400 men held nearly a third of the 3,544 directorships. This was merely one of a number of means noted by a report prepared by the Smaller War Plants Corporation last year among the devices used for concentration of controls over American economy.

These are terrifying facts. They pose the No. 1 problem before this country today. They are all the more significant when it is recognized that they do not reflect merely a static situation. They are a product of a trend which is still going on.

If what I have reported to you as to the present extent of monopoly control is startling, consider that the 200 largest nonfinancial corporations owned one-third of our national assets in 1909, 48 per cent in 1929 and 55 per cent a few years later. Consider that in 1880 the four largest producers in the iron and steel industry owned 25 per cent of the country's rolling mill capacity. In 1938 the percentage was 64. I shall not burden you with additional statistics to prove the direction in which we have been moving. There can be little dispute as to the existence of such a movement. As a result, two basic economic facts of today may be stated:

1. We are now in a situation where a small group of men controlling giant combines and combinations of interests are in a position to dictate the movement

and activities of an overwhelming portion of our entire economy.

2. The process of amalgamation, merger, and concentration is continuing today in a trend whose significance is best summarized in some recent remarks of Mr. Wendell Berge, Assistant Attorney General of the United States, in charge of antitrust prosecution, who said:

The monopoly problem is today more serious than at any time since the passage of the Sherman Act . . . The real source of the threat to free enterprise . . . lies in monopolistic control over our great industries. If we really believe what we constantly say about the necessity of preserving free enterprise then the time to act on this affirmation of belief is now . . . it is sheer delusion to believe that we can tolerate regimentation by monopoly without in time necessitating regimentation by government.

There is a peculiar irony therefore — amusing if it were not so vicious and unprincipled and so devastating potentially in its effect on the welfare of the people — in the outcries of those who call this Congress to action against the "monopoly" of labor.

At a time when small groups of men in a financial oligarchy, freed from even the relatively slight controls of legal limitations on prices are engaged in a gigantic gouge of the American people to build the profits which I have described to you,* it is suggested to this Congress that what is needed is a set of controls and curbs on the organizations of working men and women. It is suggested that we are to depart so far from the principles of the thirteenth amendment which declared that human beings

* [Editor's Note: Mr. Murray places the 1946 level of profits after taxes at $12 billion as compared with a 1936–39 average of $3.9 billion and a 1943 average of $9.9 billion.]

are not chattels, and of the Clayton Act which declared that the labor of the human being is not a commodity or article of commerce, as to declare that working men and women commit a crime against the welfare of a nation when they organize together into associations to improve the working standards and living conditions of the employees of the country.

Can such associations be likened to monopoly? I have described some of the instances and aspects of the centralization of control of our giant financial and industrial institutions. Later I propose to contrast with this the workings, objectives, and functions of a free and democratic labor organization. . . .

I would direct your attention . . . to the proposal to outlaw any coordinated collective bargaining program addressed to more than one employer in the same industry.

Let me give you one simple example before I discuss some broader implications. One of the difficult problems which has for years tormented the steel industry has been the wide variety of job titles, job rates, job duties. The industry has labored under uncoordinated, unscientific accumulations of literally thousands upon thousands of different job titles. Assigned to these jobs were rates which were merely the process of historical accumulation, not of scientific evaluation. The industry was plagued; the union was plagued. Workers were displeased with manifest inequities among their respective rates, with lower rates paid for jobs clearly higher in value than others, with varying rates paid for the same jobs in the same or related mills, and with many other respects of a complex picture without rhyme or reason.

So we, The United Steelworkers of America, representing the employees in the industry, acting pursuant to War Labor Board suggestion, sat down with representatives of major companies in the industry to solve this problem once and for all. Our representatives labored for a period not of days, not weeks, not months, but years. Within the last month the fruits of this labor insofar as the various subsidiaries of the United States Steel Corp. are involved were brought to light. The program of uniform evaluation and careful appraisal is being applied today as equitably as possible to other areas of the industry.

Industry welcomes this opportunity to bring reason and order into an area of confusion. Labor welcomes it. The bill before you would have government condemn it.

The bill has been widely designated as one to prevent industry-wide bargaining. If that were its sole effect it would be sufficiently subject to justifiable condemnation. You have already heard employers who have appeared before you to explain how valuable in their industries has been the stabilizing experience of industry-wide bargaining. It is an interesting comment that among those employers who have expressed their support for the bill before you, not one operates in an industry where industry-wide bargaining is in effect.

A recent study sponsored by Princeton University stressed the important values of industry-wide bargaining. This study concludes that this form of bargaining produces results which are "more sensible and farsighted, taking in the economic interest of the industry as a whole."

Let us recognize several basic facts in connection with this proposal: Is it calculated to promote industrial peace? It rejects any possibility of settlement of collective-bargaining relations in an industry as a result of a single major negotiation, the establishment of a pattern, or any other device calculated to promote uniformity, stability, and prompt over-all disposition of the collective-bargaining problems of the industry. All this it rejects in favor of the encouragement of hundreds or thousands of separate negotiations, separate disputes, separate strikes (if they should develop). Does that reflect progress toward industrial peace?

Is it calculated to minimize the effects of a strike upon our economy? Hasn't the war experience as well as the experience of the months succeeding the war yet established the extent to which our economy is interrelated so that it is not solely the industry-wide stoppage which impedes wide areas of production? Haven't we yet learned to realize the extent to which single stoppages can operate with bottleneck effect to impede large areas of our economy? Remember the dockmen's strike in New York City? Remember the effects of stoppages in parts plants upon major automobile production plants? Are we prepared to say it is the wise policy to prohibit generalized large-scale settlements and solutions and to insist upon scattering our problems and promoting continuous dangers of bottleneck difficulties throughout the entire year?

I cannot and do not say to you that industry-wide bargaining, so-called (and there is very little that can be said to conform to that title in major American industry today), is at all times and under all circumstances the wisest rule. I can say that in a general evaluation the considerations from the point of view of public welfare favor rather than oppose it. I can say that experience and history favor rather than oppose that type of

be the hand maidens of a market analysis more detailed, scientific, and exhaustive than ever before. Both managements and unions need definitive data superior to that which they now usually possess.

In connection with the proposal for curtailing unions as monopolies, it is of interest to note the nature of the UAW Constitution with reference to bargaining procedure.

Article 19, section 2 provides that "... a committee selected by the local union shall participate in all conferences and negotiations." Section 3 of this article stipulates that: "No local union officer, international officer or international representative shall have the authority to negotiate the terms of a contract or any supplement thereof with any employer without first obtaining the approval of the local union." It then goes on to provide for approval by the International only after local union approval. Section 4 reads: "National agreements and supplements thereof shall be ratified by the local unions involved."

Section 5 reads: "The general meeting of the local union members of a manufacturing establishment under the jurisdiction of an amalgamated local union (one embracing more than one manufacturing establishment) shall be the highest authority for handling problems within the manufacturing establishment. ... Article 20 provides for an intracorporation council, in cases of bargaining with multiplant corporations such as GM. These councils, whose elected representatives are voted for by the local membership on a per capita basis, guide and participate in the negotiations in such cases.

Turning to the procedure in the event of strike action, an equally democratic process is involved which also is governed by the majority decision of the local union membership. . . .

The citation of these provisions should make it clear that control of collective bargaining, negotiations and strike action in the UAW-CIO stems from the workers in the shop, and that decisions on these matters are made primarily on the plant level in each case. Demands to curb monopoly and dictatorship in unions find no foundation in facts as they pertain to the auto workers.

I might add parenthetically that had we achieved industry-wide bargaining in the auto industry we would have avoided certain strikes which took place during the last year for the purpose of obtaining for the membership of other local unions the wage increase won in General Motors. Stoppages resulted from the absence of industry-wide disposition of this issue, as is the case with reference to every basic demand of common interest to all workers in the industry.

Finally, I should point out that no action is being taken, or is apparently contemplated, by this Congress to break up big corporations such as General Motors and United States Steel on the ground that they are (quoting a Detroit News, Feb. 13, report of an interview with Senator Ball in Grand Rapids, Mich.): ". . . too big for their own good and for the public good." Unless and until such action is taken it cannot in fairness be suggested that their opposite numbers, large industrial unions, should be subjected to fragmentation.

John L. Lewis · UNITED MINE WORKERS

THE National Association of Manufacturers, the National United States Chamber of Commerce, the National Coal Association, and various individual industrialists and employers are very ardently advocating restrictions on what they call industry-wide bargaining. This is one of the most flagrant proposals against the right of workers to exercise their basic rights that has been proposed in the Congress.

Significantly, the recommendations come from those who are enjoying the benefits of national organization and national association. Their thinking along these lines seems to run to the proposition that if the workers can be put in irons to the extent that they can be prevented from exercising the benefits of collective action, while at the same time they have such benefits themselves, that with this power granted to them by the State, they can isolate the labor unions into small groups and by pincers movements destroy them.

These proposals completely ignore the dignity and rights of labor as human beings and treats them as chattel slaves. They repeal the passage of the Clayton Act that recognizes that the labor of human beings is not a commodity or article of commerce.

The charge that the labor unions have secured a monopoly upon certain industries is a red herring drawn across the track in order to divert the interest of the people from the real monopoly created by the corporations during and since the war. The concentration during

the war period is graphically demonstrated by the fact that two thirds of the 175 billion dollars of Government contracts awarded from June, 1940 through September, 1944 went to the 100 largest firms in the Nation. In fact, almost one half of the value of the contracts went to the 30 top corporations, one corporation alone obtaining 14 billion dollars on contracts. During the war period, in contrast, more than half a million small businesses disappeared entirely.

Looking at it from another angle, of the Nation's total manufacturing facilities of 40 billion dollars, 250 corporations owned about 30 billion dollars before the war. The war added about 26 billion dollars, with the Government putting up 18 billion dollars. Most of the new Government-financed facilities, now known as surplus plants, are going to the bigger business concerns.

Examination of the list of 250 giant corporations discloses that 30 of the very largest which control almost one third of the Nation's manufacturing facilities are dominated or controlled by 5 banking groups. Four of these groups head up in New York, the fifth in Cleveland.

Much has been said by certain representatives of the coal industry about industry-wide collective bargaining. These representatives have tried to paint a picture of labor domination of an industry that is detrimental to the employers and to the public. Let us look at the record.

During the war years, 1941 through VJ-day, the coal miners in this country produced more coal with less men than

From Hearings on S. 55 and S. J. Res. 22, Committee on Labor and Public Welfare, United States Senate, 80th Congress, 1st Session, part 4, March 1947, pp. 1992–1996, 2018–2019. Also from testimony of John L. Lewis before the House of Representatives Subcommittee on Miner's Welfare of the Committee on Education and Labor. April 3, 1947.

all of the rest of the nations in the world combined, including the Axis nations. Without the necessity of utilizing vast sums of money derived from taxation and taken from the public purse, the coal industry with its manpower depleted by hundreds and thousands of men, with restrictions placed upon it by inadequacy of supplies, interruptions of production which came from causes for which the industry was not to blame, the coal industry supplied the Nation and moved excess tonnage to other countries. That feat and that accomplishment, unparalleled in economic history of this country or any other, has gone unsung. No medals have been handed out to the men in the coal industry either for working or for dying — and many have died.

When final figures of 1946 production are tabulated, bituminous production will total approximately 535,000,000 tons, with anthracite production around 61,000,000 tons, for a combined total of 596,000,000 tons. This huge total was produced by a daily working force averaging 475,000 men. Production for the week ending January 11, 1947, as reported by the Solid Fuels Administration, was 13,700,000 tons of bituminous coal, the highest week's output in 20 years. There has never been such a production record achieved before in industrial history in any country.

A minimum of 15,000,000 tons was lost in production due to the railroad-car shortage, which continues to exist and which is now causing a weekly production loss of 1,000,000 tons.

Contrast that record with the production in the United Kingdom of Great Britain which for decades past, next to our own country, has been the ranking producer of coal of all character. English production for 1946, with an employ-ment of 695,000 miners, approximates 183,000,000 tons.

The American coal miner produces more tons per man than any coal miner in the world. The consumer in America receives the cheapest coal of any consumer of any nation in the world, and yet this achievement goes unsung in the public press, in the councils of certain coal operators, and in the councils of Government it has been totally ignored.

Coal is produced at a rate hitherto deemed impossible, but at what a price in human agony, in human sorrow, in shortened lives, deprivation of opportunity on the part of countless human beings, victims of the unjust and improper conditions under which they serve and whom it is proposed shall be restricted in their right to bargain collectively to alleviate these conditions.

Coal miners have been little rewarded. They received only 18½ cents increase in wages as applied to their basic hourly rate since 1941. They were permitted to work more time, which they gladly did. They were permitted to have pay for travel time, which hitherto had been denied them. The fact that they were permitted to work more days and more hours, and receive pay for something they had been doing without pay, was considered by some people of this country a great favor to coal miners. Our coal miners are now working a deadly, brutal 54-hour workweek underground in American coal mines. Our miners work at the operators' option 9 hours per day, 6 days per week, which is a longer workday or workweek than prevails in the mining industry of any other civilized country in the world.

Certainly Senators should ponder this remarkable achievement on the part of freemen and free citizens. They should repudiate any attempt at restricting these American workers by refusing to listen to the ill-informed antiunion elements who are proposing such a fantastic restriction upon the rights of American workmen who have so splendidly served their country in war and are now serving it in peace to an extent unequaled in history.

* * *

SENATOR AIKEN. I have one question, Mr. Lewis.

This committee, as you well know, is under constant pressure to enact legislation to prevent strikes in those industries upon which the economy of the country depends, and we are given as examples the coal industry, power industry, and the railroads. Do you believe that any legislation which the Congress might enact would successfully guarantee the constant production of coal?

MR. LEWIS. Senator, I am convinced beyond doubt that such legislation would not be successful, so long as we seek to retain our form of government.

There are 60,000,000 people gainfully employed in the United States now. This miracle age, as far as material science is concerned, is changing the form of employment in America. A lesser number of people are employed in the production of food on the farms. We have some 7,000,000 families or 21,000,000 people in agriculture. We have 60,000,000 people gainfully employed, working by hand or brain, in America's productive enterprises. They live in urban communities. They are dependent upon economic production for their existence. I do not know how in a free economy you can enact a law and preserve freedom for private investment and for other citizens and force 60,000,000 people to abandon their right to stop working collectively. In order to do so, the Congress would

have to give the executive branch of the Government such a grant of authority and build up such tremendous powers that the Republic would no longer exist. Those powers would not be exercised in the hands of those gainfully employed. They would be exercised in the hands of oppressive government and would fall on the other class of the population.

SENATOR AIKEN. It is your contention that under our form of government industrial peace cannot be guaranteed by law?

MR. LEWIS. I do not know how in a competitive system you can compel a seller to sell or a buyer to buy. Certainly, under our system a man can sell his goods or withhold them. These 60,000,000 people have nothing to sell except the labor of their hands or the labor of their brains. Certainly, they have an equal right under our Constitution, under our concept of Government, to sell that service, or withhold it. And if the Congress should enact a law denying that right, which I think is inherent in the Constitution, then, certainly the Congress is changing the form of government, because merely enforcement of that law is going to create bodies of men embittered by the exploitation of ruthless employers. The enforcement of that law, in my judgment, would be quite a task and more confusing to Americans in America than the present situation.

What happens now? We have built up a high standard of living. Our investors get a return. The 1946 records show that. It was the best of all years. Nobody has been hurt. The workers as a whole, on the average, have the highest standards of any nation in the world, the highest that ever existed before.

Of course, there are inequities in it. Of course, there are peaks and valleys in it.

All right. We are doing the job of production and reserving the right to contend with each other as to what our share of participation in the increased efficiency will be. Is not that the American way?

THE CHAIRMAN [Senator Taft]. The question, though, Mr. Lewis, is whether you can tie up the whole country, throw steel workers, and hundreds of thousands of other workers out of work, because you and the mine operators cannot agree. I mean I do not think it is the same as one man quitting work, having the right to quit work. But, when you have a large organization like yours quitting work I think we have to look for a remedy.

MR. LEWIS. Would not the alternative be the fair treatment of the coal miners on the part of whatever authority exists, whether it is the Government or the coal operators?

THE CHAIRMAN. I do not think you can say it is unfair nor can we say you are unfair for what you ask for. That is not the question. It is perfectly reasonable that you and the employer should disagree at times, and that collective bargaining may finally break down. That is true in any industry. The question is should we undertake to impose compulsory arbitration or other Government action to determine what the justice of the situation is and then use the power of the Government as they are using it in the present situation, to try to carry that out?

MR. LEWIS. Well, it is a question, whether you want to create liberty or security.

THE CHAIRMAN. Up to a point, but there is a point at which that failure, if it starves the rest of the Nation, for instance, or freezes the rest of the Nation, cuts all the rest of the plants off in the Nation, it seems to me the Government may have to do something about it. That is the difficulty I have.

MR. LEWIS. I point out that the Nation has never yet starved, frozen, or died from want of water. The restraints as affecting labor are the inherent restraints that affect all America. We have no guaranties in our country what a school board will do or a city council or a State legislature, or the Federal Congress, or a labor union, or the Baptist Church, or some other church, or the Kiwanis Club, or the Farm Federation. We have no guaranties that those organizations will not act wrongfully.

We have, however, enough confidence in the fairness of the average man in his desire to do the right thing to believe that this Republic that we have created, with those inherent individual restraints, can continue to function.

THE CHAIRMAN. Do you think you are an average man, though, Mr. Lewis? In most industries there are several thousand people that make the decisions. Apparently, in coal it is practically up to you individually.

MR. LEWIS. I wonder why you make an inaccurate statement like that.

THE CHAIRMAN. That is a fact.

MR. LEWIS. I wonder why you create a premise there and then talk from that premise when it is inaccurate.

THE CHAIRMAN. Is it not true of an international union of this kind, rightfully or wrongfully — they may be right or they may be wrong in their contention — they do have the power to shut down the entire country? They are not average men, therefore. They are powerful men.

MR. LEWIS. Senator, I too have read in the paper that you are pushing the Republican Party about and making decisions.

THE CHAIRMAN. Let me say this.

MR. LEWIS. I was fair enough and

tolerant enough to withhold judgment on that until I could talk to you.

THE CHAIRMAN. In this Congress no man can boss anybody.

MR. LEWIS. That is true in any union, too.

THE CHAIRMAN. No man can get the agreement of every Senator and House Member unless they want to agree. My impression is — I may be wrong — you can pretty well run the United Mine Workers yourself.

MR. LEWIS. I want to say this. The men who compose the United Mine Workers are just about the same kind of men, inherently and basically, that comprise the Republican Party in the United States Senate or the Democratic Party, or the Kiwanis Club.

So, I do not think your suggestion to me that I can tie up the country is a valid one, because it simply does not work out in real life and it is not true. I do not know anybody that can induce anybody else to go on strike against his will. I do not know why anyone would want to induce anyone to go on strike against his will. As a matter of fact, most of the authority I exercise is trying to terminate strikes after they are started. I did that on December 7, did I not? I have done it before. I may do it again tomorrow.

My influence to do so merely depends upon the degree of confidence which the mine workers in this country hold in me. That is all. I only have moral persuasion. I have no arbitrary power over any man.

THE CHAIRMAN. Senator Ball.

SENATOR BALL. Mr. Lewis, can I pursue this question on industry-wide shutdown a little further? I think you would recognize that industry-wide shut-down in the production of coal has terrific repercussions on our economy. You have very vividly told us that the production

of coal has gone up. We are an economy dependent upon power, and every time there is a prolonged strike affecting the total coal production its secondary effects are tremendous. Last year there were millions of people not directly involved who were out of work because plants slowed down and production stopped.

Do you not think there is a point where the exercise of the right and freedom by one group of individuals impinges so drastically on the rights, privileges, and freedoms of all others that the Government has to step in and do something about it?

MR. LEWIS. No, I think definitely the Government should not, Senator, not if you want to preserve America as we know it, and its freedom, because you cannot regulate the human beings who work for a living in this country, and who in a major sense are not rich and in a substantial sense are quite poor. You cannot regulate them and leave everyone else free to do as they will, to hold their commodities or what not. You would have to have a nation that was automatically regulated in its every action. I do not think you can.

Senator, do you not agree with me that the country has never yet been frozen, that the country has never yet been discommoded, that the country has never yet suffered irreparable injury from deprivation of coal or anything else, that every strike and every lock-out carries with it the seeds of its own determination, that the restraints that are inherent on the individual will operate within the mass, and in the union, and in the economy of the country? Those are simply prices we pay for preserving free enterprise and liberty.

You cannot harness 600,000 people and say you cannot strike now except under the regulations of the Congress;

you cannot work except under the regulations of Congress, because you would not be able to get me to go in the coal mines under those circumstances.

I would like to point out in passing that that is a problem which will be very acute in the future. We are not getting manpower in the mines. Our young men are not going in the mines. They do not have to. They find better conditions in other industries, and they are not going in.

The older men are dying off, being killed, and injured. There are 65,000 injuries a year, 2,000 deaths, 2,000 total disabilities, 25,000 partial disabilities, 1 man in every 6 injured or killed each year in the coal mines; every man in the coal industry killed or injured every 6 years statistically. They work 9 hours a day underground, which is too long, and 6 days a week. The wages of the coal miner are less than the dressmaker in New York. They have a 35-hour week in the women's garment trade in New York at a higher wage per week than the coal miner has at a 54-hour week.

So, I am pointing out that the question of preserving our ability to produce coal in America depends upon our ability to give fair treatment to these men, so they will remain in the mines and so we can get other men to go in the mines.

SENATOR BALL. I have no argument with you on that. I would agree with you that so far we have not frozen. We came pretty close to it up in some of the Northern States a couple of times when the coal supplies were shut off. We were

certainly discommoded. Many millions of people have been as a result of these shut-downs.

As you, yourself, have reason to know very well, there has been tremendous pressure on Government to take very drastic action. The President proposed a drastic action in order to get coal, to keep the railroads running. I think that kind of compulsion would really mean the end of individual freedom. I think we must find some way of limiting the effects of strikes. I agree with you that we cannot have a free economy and not preserve the right to strike. I think you can preserve the right and limit it considerably beyond what we have so far.

It seems to me that is a sounder answer than just leaving the country at the mercy of these industry-wide shut-downs, and if they become severe enough, and we cannot guarantee the operators will agree with you and that the steel industry will agree with Mr. Murray, and if you get these prolonged shut-downs, you are going to get pressure for more action and you are going to get a compulsory arbitration for the industry to which I am opposed just as much as you are.

MR. LEWIS. Senator, I do not want to ask a question, but I must say it more or less in an interrogatory.

Would it not be advantageous to keep all of those fearsome things away from us that you paint by merely starting in to give the miners decent treatment so they will not have any incentive to stop work or strike?

INDUSTRIAL EXPERIENCES WITH
INDUSTRY–WIDE BARGAINING

George W. Taylor and Waldo E. Fisher · COLLECTIVE
BARGAINING IN THE BITUMINOUS COAL INDUSTRY:
AN APPRAISAL

INTRODUCTION by *George W. Taylor*

TO many persons, the problem of industry-wide bargaining is virtually synonymous with the problem of labor relations in the bituminous coal industry. Simultaneous shut-downs of all coal mines, and successive threats of such stoppages, have sharply focused the attention of the entire nation upon the great social costs which have to be paid when industry-wide collective bargaining fails to produce peacefully negotiated agreements.

In concentrating attention upon this particular cost of industry-wide bargaining — a cost which can be oppressively heavy — there is a disposition to conclude too readily that all would be well if only industry-wide bargaining were replaced by bargaining less inclusive in coverage. This delusion is possible only because memories are short. Mine-by-mine bargaining, or multi-employer bargaining covering only a part of the coal industry, for that matter, would entail other heavy social costs and bring oppressive burdens to coal miners and coal operators alike. There need be no conjecture about these points. They were starkly highlighted in the experience of earlier days.

Waldo E. Fisher's careful and well-documented study of collective bargain-ing in the bituminous coal industry gives a much-needed historical perspective against which the current problems of that industry can be properly appraised. The record of the past moreover, must be kept clearly in mind whenever the "coal problem" is under discussion, particularly if proposed solutions to current problems are to be practical and equitable.

In recounting the very early history of the coal industry, for example, Dr. Fisher shows "the utter helplessness of the individual employee and employer in the face of economic forces and conditions that prevail in an overdeveloped industry." Successive price wars were accompanied by a series of drastic wage reductions. The consequent chaos re-sulted, as early as 1886, in joint efforts by the union and by the operators to introduce some measure of wage stability in the industry. Multi-employer bargaining was looked to as the most practical way of avoiding really ruinous competition and a serious disorganization of one of the country's most vital industries.

Until recent years, the various efforts to institute multi-employer bargaining in bituminous coal had to be limited to only a part of the industry. The results, and

From *Collective Bargaining in the Bituminous Coal Industry: An Appraisal* by George W. Taylor and Waldo E. Fisher. Wharton School of Finance and Commerce, University of Pennsylvania Press, 1948. Reprinted by permission.

particularly the economic consequences of this particular form of bargaining, are carefully appraised by Dr. Fisher in his analysis of collective bargaining in the Central Competitive Field. It is shown that competitive advantages retained by unorganized mines gave non-union operators a dominant control over costs and prices. The attempt to stabilize wages and working conditions for a part of the industry was vitiated every time sales and employment declined. Those experiences verified the conclusion of many economists that successful collective bargaining in the coal industry "must embrace substantially all producing fields serving common markets."

The notable study made by Waldo Fisher shows how the organization of employees and of operators for virtually industry-wide bargaining in the coal industry was impelled by powerful economic forces and sought to meet human problems of paramount importance. The adoption of industry-wide bargaining was an effort to control pressures that, if not checked, could bring disastrous results to the industry and to the country. The study also sharply delineates the new and formidable problems that arose out of the program for meeting the problems of mine-by-mine bargaining. It is suggested in the study that industry-wide bargaining can be successful only if the parties to this relationship "assume their responsibilities to each other and the public, relate their demands to the realities of economic life, and share the gains of progress not only among themselves, but with the public." In a larger sense, there are the necessities for collective bargaining in general.

The monograph which Waldo Fisher has prepared, on the basis of his close study of the bituminous coal industry over many years, is a major contribution to the literature of industrial relations. It will undoubtedly prove to be of incalculable value in the development of an understanding about industry-wide bargaining in general and about the industrial relations of the coal industry in particular.

SUMMARY by *Waldo E. Fisher*

What conclusions may be drawn from this economic analysis of collective bargaining in the bituminous coal industry?

The history of labor relations in bituminous coal shows the utter helplessness of the individual employee and employer in the face of economic forces and conditions that prevail in an over-developed industry. In any highly competitive industry in which the establishments are many and widely decentralized, and supply common markets, collective bargaining under capable leadership is necessary not only to protect workers and maintain decent standards of living, but also to safeguard employers' investments.

Experience with labor relations in this industry also verifies the contention of economists that successful collective bargaining must embrace substantially all producing fields serving common markets. The failure of the Central Competitive Field Compact must be laid largely to union inability to organize the southern fields. No system of collective bargaining can long work if one group of employers must pay rigid wage scales and meet union standards of employment, while another group conducts its business under flexible wage scales and working conditions arrived at through individual bargaining. Under such conditions the non-union employers control both costs and prices and can therefore dominate the market.

Once an industry, for practical purposes, is completely organized, the union is in a very strong bargaining position. The threat of non-union competition is gone. There is no one left within the industry to undersell the union operations and take away their markets. Moreover, the will to resist union demands on the part of the operators is greatly weakened, since the increased costs occasioned by such demands can more easily be passed on to the public. Competition with substitute products is, of course, a restraining factor, but in this industry it has not been a very effective force since 1940, nor is it likely to be in the next few years. Under these conditions, organized workers can push up wages materially and secure greatly improved conditions of employment with relatively little resistance. Recent developments in this industry have demonstrated the truth of this statement.

A collective bargaining arrangement can be made to work in an industry in which one union has brought into its organization most of the employees in the industry. How well it will work will depend upon the economic statesmanship of the representatives of the two parties. If both parties will assume their responsibilities to each other and the public, relate their demands to the realities of economic life, and share the gains of progress not only among themselves but with the public, industry-wide bargaining can be successful. If the employers fail to resist with courage uneconomic and unreasonable demands of labor organizations, then the system may succeed, but at the expense of the consumer. If labor leaders insist upon getting all the traffic will bear and disregard the right to share in scientific discoveries and technological improvements, industry-wide collective bargaining will fail to function in the interest of society as a whole, and organized labor will benefit at the expense of the public and probably the employers. The resulting higher costs and prices, sooner or later, will bring into play compensating economic forces — greatly intensified mechanization, product substitution, and better utilization of product — which will exact their toll in the form of a reduction in demand and reduced employment opportunity.

Richard A. Lester and Edward A. Robie · WAGES UNDER NATIONAL AND REGIONAL COLLECTIVE BARGAINING: EXPERIENCE IN SEVEN INDUSTRIES

... EXPERIENCE with uniform wage scales under national or regional collective bargaining in seven manufacturing industries is examined in this report. Bituminous and anthracite coal, the railroads, and other service industries were not included because the primary purpose of the study was to analyze the experience in manufacturing and to discover the problems and probable success that would be likely to attend attempts to achieve wage uniformity through re-

From *Wages under National and Regional Collective Bargaining* by Richard A. Lester and Edward A. Robie. Industrial Relations Section, Department of Economics and Social Institutions, Princeton University, 1946. Reprinted by permission.

gional and national collective bargaining in large manufacturing industries. The study, therefore, emphasizes factors that tend to disrupt wage equality under multiple-employer bargaining as well as factors that encourage or reinforce wage uniformity. . . .

In selecting the specific industries for study, two criteria were stressed: (1) a sufficiently long period of experience with standard industry rates under national or regional bargaining, and (2) a wide variation in the economic circumstances and experience of the selected industries, so that instructive comparisons could be made.

The first three industries discussed (pressed and blown glassware, pottery, and stoves) have had 45 to 55 years of experience with national bargaining, during which wage reductions have at times been negotiated. American Federation of Labor unions are involved; wage uniformity has developed around a system of piece rates for skilled workers; and the need for wage standardization to help stabilize the industry has been a factor in the adoption and maintenance of national bargaining. The area of wage uniformity, however, has been contracting in stoves while expanding in flint glassware and pottery.

The circumstances are more varied in the other four industries, which have had experience with national or regional bargaining for ten to fifteen years. All except pulp and paper are organized by CIO unions. Time rates are the only method of payment in silk and rayon dyeing and finishing and in West Coast pulp and paper. In flat glass and the Pacific Coast pulp and paper, one or two large firms dominate an "industry" that has a relatively low ratio of labor costs to total manufacturing costs, so that there is little need for market-wide wage standards in order to stabilize the industry. In most of the industries there is only one employers' association, while rayon and silk dyeing and finishing has seven. Flat glass and dyeing and finishing employ mostly unskilled and semi-skilled labor, whereas skilled workers constitute almost two-thirds of the labor force in full-fashioned hosiery.

Negotiation by representatives of a number of employers whose plants are scattered over a region of the country or throughout the country is the essence of regional and national collective bargaining. The distinction between national and regional bargaining is sometimes difficult to draw in specific cases. Obviously, a pulp and paper program confined to the West Coast is regional bargaining. Less obvious is the case of full-fashioned hosiery, where the employers' association with which the union bargains includes mills from Massachusetts to California, yet all of them are located in the North and have represented only 20 to 35 per cent of the industry's total equipment. It was the non-union southern competition that forced temporary abandonment of the uniform piece-rate system for three years in full-fashioned hosiery. The bargaining unit in stoves is also confined to 20 per cent of the industry and to plants located in the North. In the other five industries, however, the multi-employer negotiations, with the union cover 70 to 90 per cent of the industry's total output, including some southern plants in the case of flat glass and flint glassware. A total of about 112,000 workers are directly covered by national or regional bargaining in the seven industries. . . .

Only tentative conclusions can be drawn from experience in but seven industries, especially since national or regional bargaining began for three of them after 1933 and has not, therefore, been tested by severe business depression and widespread wage reductions. Nevertheless, the experience examined seems sufficiently varied and representative to permit qualified answers to such questions as the following: Is national or regional bargaining on wages feasible under a wide variety of circumstances? Under national or regional bargaining, is uniformity in wage scales either necessary or inevitable? What factors encourage wage uniformity and what difficulties or problems arise in attempting to maintain such wage uniformity? What are the economic effects of national and regional wage bargaining?

A. Feasibility under Varied Circumstances

1. National bargaining on wages is practicable in an industry with plants scattered throughout the country including the South. The full-fashioned hosiery mills in the employers' association are distributed from Massachusetts to California and in small communities as well as large cities; both flat and flint glass plants in the South are included within the national bargaining units in those industries.

2. Although national and regional bargaining can aid materially in stabilizing highly competitive industries with a large ratio of labor costs to total manufacturing costs, such a situation is not a prerequisite for successful national or regional bargaining on wages. One or two firms dominate flat glass and West Coast pulp and paper and in both of them labor costs are only 25 or 30 per cent of total manufacturing costs.

3. The piece-rate method of payment is not essential for multiple-employer bargaining on wages. Time rates are the exclusive method of payment in West Coast pulp and paper, in silk and rayon dyeing and finishing, and (except for cutters in window glass plants) in flat glass.

4. Uniform wage scales between firms are neither a prerequisite for, nor an inevitable result of, national or regional bargaining on wages. (See below, Section B.)

5. Neither job evaluation nor standard job classifications are required for multiple-employer bargaining on wages. In some of the seven industries (e.g. hosiery and pottery), wage rates are far out of line with any objective evaluation of the jobs; in the machine printing and plain dyeing branch of the silk and rayon dyeing and finishing industry, the same minimum rate applies to about 90 per cent of the workers. None of the seven industries has a uniform system of job classification except West Coast paper and pulp. An attempt was made to establish such a system in stoves in 1945.

6. National bargaining can be carried on without the whole industry being organized or without having all organized firms participate in the negotiations. In no case studied were all firms in the industry included in the bargaining unit. Although only around 20 per cent of the stove and hosiery industries, and about 50 per cent of the china branch in pottery, are direct participants in the national system, the pattern of wage changes thus negotiated generally spreads throughout most of the industry. This is especially true in hosiery and china.

7. National or regional bargaining can start with a few important occupations and gradually spread to others. That, for example, has been the process of evolution in pottery, hosiery, flint glass, and stoves.

B. Wage Uniformity Not Essential

1. In Sweden and England a pattern of geographic wage differentials has been developed in most industries under national collective bargaining.

2. A fixed pattern of wage differentials, based on criteria generally considered fair and acceptable, has arisen under national bargaining in some industries in this country. Three separate schedules and levels of wages have developed for the same jobs (including skilled maintenance crafts) in hand, combination, and automatic-machine plants in flint glass, and agreements in silk and rayon dyeing and finishing allow ten per cent under the metropolitan scale for outlying areas (like upstate New York and eastern Pennsylvania), as a fair measure of the distance handicap.

3. Inter-firm differentials may also be maintained under national bargaining. That has been true in flat glass and for one firm that gave an independent wage increase in flint glass.

4. Uniform wage scales may apply to some piece-rate occupations, while for other jobs the rate varies from plant to plant. For example, the National Labor Agreement in full-fashioned hosiery leaves time rates for local determination, requiring payment of local prevailing rates for certain occupations, and in flint glass the time rates are only minima, with actual wage payments considerably higher for some firms and in some localities. The pottery industry, particularly the china branch, has numerous occupations for which rates are determined locally.

5. Wage rates paid for the same product or occupation may differ because the equipment, materials, or other job conditions vary between plants or within a plant. "Extra" payments over the uniform scale are required in hosiery and pottery, and higher hourly or piece rates are permitted for non-standard jobs in hosiery, flint glass, and West Coast pulp and paper.

6. The national unions and most employers covered under national or regional bargaining usually favor practical uniformity of wage scales or standards for the industry. Not only is the principle of the same pay for equal work considered fair by the unions but, through national bargaining, they seek to prevent undercutting of rates by eliminating wage competition between firms. The chief advantages of national or regional bargaining from the point of view of employers also arise from substantial equality in wage scales: stabilization of costs in the industry, elimination of pace-setting by a wage "leader" or "whip-sawing" by the union playing one firm against another, and removal of wage differentials based on differences in the wage-paying ability of individual firms.

* * *

D. Economic Effects

1. Under national or regional bargaining, wage decisions are likely to be more sensible and far-sighted, taking into consideration the economic interests of the industry as a whole, than is the case where the wage pattern for the industry is established by a wage "leader" or by local bargaining, with the union playing one firm against another. Experience (e.g., West Coast pulp and paper in 1940) indicates that the union's wage demands may be more modest when they apply uniformly and simultaneously to all plants in a multiple-employer unit. Illustrative also of the tendency for responsibility and caution to prevail under national and regional bargaining

are the warnings of the Hosiery Workers' officials in 1946 against "irrational opportunism" in a temporary boom.

2. Generally speaking, wage and earning levels do not appear to have risen more rapidly under national and regional bargaining than for manufacturing as a whole. That, for example, appears to be true for flint glass, pottery, hosiery, silk and rayon dyeing and finishing, and probably for stoves although adequate data are not available for purposes of comparison. Indeed, the level in pottery from 1912 to 1929 and in hosiery during the 1930's rose less than that for all manufacturing, and in silk and rayon dyeing and finishing wage rates remained the same for six and a half years following December, 1934. Wages in West Coast pulp and paper have risen somewhat relative to the industry in the rest of the country but, at times, the increase in the related lumber industry has exceeded that in pulp and paper on the Coast. And although the increases in flat glass have been greater than for manufacturing in general, they have tended to parallel those in neighboring steel and aluminum industries. Obviously no conclusions can be drawn for the period of Federal wage control during World War II.

3. Levels of wages in the seven industries taken as a group are not high; for some occupations or areas the rates are relatively high and for some comparatively low. On the basis of job requirements, flat glass wages are relatively high both for the South, and also for window glass cutters. The pay of maintenance workers is high in West Coast pulp and paper, particularly in view of the stability of employment they have enjoyed. The hourly earnings are comparatively high for some skilled jobs in full-fashioned hosiery and are exceptionally high for some unskilled jobs (such as sweeper) in silk and rayon dyeing and finishing. On the other hand, hourly wages are comparatively low in the lowest-paying jobs in flint glass and hosiery, and are not relatively high for some of the semi-skilled and skilled jobs in silk and rayon dyeing and finishing.

4. Wage patterns under national and regional collective bargaining apparently have not served to place any additional restraint on technological improvement and new investment. At least that seems to have been the case in such industries as pottery, flat glass, and, during recent years, in full-fashioned hosiery. In 1938 an arbitrator reported that some hosiery piece rates were obsolete and restrictive. In flint glass, some employers have complained that failure to vary the piece rates with differences in equipment has tended to retard the introduction of improved techniques. Experience in hosiery and pottery indicates that the rate structure under national bargaining can be adjusted to eliminate any such retarding effect.

5. Monopolistic or collusive practices with regard to wages or economic change have not characterized any of the seven industries. Indeed, elimination of wage-cutting has tended to stress efficiency of management as the most important factor in competition. The anti-trust case in flat glass has not concerned collective bargaining. In silk and rayon dyeing and finishing, union officials apparently have been making sincere efforts to loosen up pre-existing limitations upon output by individual employees. In adopting a policy of uniform wage scales, the union gives up the possibility of monopolistic price discrimination — fixing wages according to each employer's ability to pay.

6. Under national and regional bargaining, wages do tend to be somewhat

more stable and rigid than under local bargaining. Group bargaining and national agreements may serve as a brake on wage movements both upward and downward. Wage uniformity, with a scale of wages contained in the national agreement, tends to reduce wage flexibility between occupations, between firms, and between localities. Such a tendency can, however, be considerably modified by such means as specifying only minimum rates for some occupations (as in pottery, flint glass, and silk and rayon dyeing and finishing), allowing firms to have varied incentive systems (as in flint and flat glass and in silk and rayon dyeing and finishing), permitting alternative methods of payment for some jobs (as in pottery), providing for special pay for non-standard jobs (as in flint glass and full-fashioned hosiery), or omitting certain jobs from the agreement (as in pottery and hosiery). The most rigid wage set-up discussed in this report is that in West Coast pulp and paper.

7. Local interests and the interests of smaller firms have generally been well represented in wage negotiations under national or regional bargaining in the seven industries. In the employers' associations, each firm has one vote in flint glass and each mill has one vote in West Coast pulp and paper. On the union side, the proposed wage scale is submitted to a referendum of the membership in all covered locals in the case of hosiery, West Coast pulp and paper, and two branches of flint glass. The most unsatisfactory situations from the point of view of representation of minority interests are flat glass, where prior negotiations with the two big companies tend to establish the wage pattern for "Little Glass," and silk and rayon dyeing and finishing, where the nature of the industry and the division among employers places a large part of the wage-determining power in a highly centralized union.

8. The friction and labor strife involved in changes in money wage levels may be reduced through national or regional bargaining, judging by the experience in these seven industries. Concentration of the change in one industry-wide determination avoids the labor unrest and series of strikes that often accompany competition between firms in the timing of wage changes or competition between rival unions in exacting concessions from employers. . . . Labor relations in the seven industries have been relatively peaceful.

Almon E. Roth · NATIONAL FEDERATION OF AMERICAN SHIPPING

WE are convinced that it would be impracticable and inadvisable to prohibit area- or industry-wide bargaining in the shipping industry, for the following reasons:

The enactment of this bill would annul practically every important collective-bargaining agreement in the maritime industry. The ensuing result would be utter chaos in collective bargaining and innumerable jurisdictional disputes. In this connection we should like to point to the following facts which are peculiar to shipping operations.

From Testimony on S. 55 and S. J. Res. 22, Committee on Labor and Public Welfare, United States Senate, 80th Congress, 1st Session, part 2, February 1947.

Many shipping operations are conducted on a world-wide basis, and practically all shipping operations are conducted over an area which is more extensive than that included in the exemption set forth in this bill.

I have already pointed out that the Government prescribes the minimum number of crew members in various classifications who must be on board as a condition to sailing the vessel. The place of employment of a vessel is not localized. There is little continuity of employment. In most cases the men sign on for one voyage only, and are continually shifting from one ship to another and from one employer to another. In the course of the voyage it frequently is necessary to sign on new crew members at various ports in order to meet Government requirements. Crews and replacements are obtained from union hiring halls which have been established in the principal ports. Under such circumstances you can well imagine how impracticable it would be for each ship operator to deal individually with a union which represents only his own employees. The seamen, in order to be assured of any continuity of employment, would have to belong to innumerable individual local unions.

This bill would mean that each steamship company would have to stand by itself and act separately from all others in dealing with the offshore unions. We know, to our sorrow, from past experience what the results would be. There would be a diversity of wage rates and working conditions among ships operated from the same coast, plying between the same ports, tying at the same docks, and employing in turn the same men. Experience has shown that such a condition leads to the playing off of one steamship company against another by the unions, to extreme labor unrest, and eventually to the disruption of steamship operation.

The same sort of problem is presented in respect to shoreside employees. The steamship companies are the direct employers of most dock workers other than longshoremen. In the case of longshoremen, a stevedoring contractor usually intervenes, but longshore labor is so vital to steamship operations that steamship companies, to protect themselves, have found it necessary to join as parties to the collective bargaining contract with the longshoremen's union in many ports. In all ports longshoremen and other dock workers are for the most part casual employees who work for one steamship company or stevedore and then another as their services are required to meet the fluctuations of work at the different docks. It would be utterly impractical, to put it mildly, for each steamship company and stevedore to deal separately with the union and to fix wages, hours, and working conditions independently of the other employers. They would not be protected by the provision permitting joint bargaining within a hundred-mile area for the simple reason, if for no other, that many longshoremen and other dock employees work beyond a hundred-mile area. Thus, for example, longshoremen are dispatched from Seattle to various outlying ports, several of which are more than a hundred miles away. Similarly longshoremen are dispatched from Portland to various outlying ports more than a hundred miles away.

The provisions of this bill would not preclude the possibility of area-wide or nation-wide strikes in the shipping industry. Only last fall we witnessed a nation-wide tie-up of shipping which was in no way related to industry-wide bargaining. Our nation-wide maritime strike of last September was caused by sympathy strikes by a number of individual unions in support of a strike by the sailors' union of the Pacific against a ruling by the NLRB. The reluctance of maritime labor to work behind the picket line, even though it may be established by a rival union, makes it possible for any local union to tie up an entire port or even shipping on a much wider area.

The experience of both Great Britain and Sweden, as well as our own experience in the railroad industry, demonstrates that area-wide or national strikes cannot be charged against industry-wide bargaining. As previously stated, there has not been an offshore maritime strike of any consequence in British shipping in more than 20 years.

We doubt whether the prohibition against industry-wide bargaining would impair the strength of unions or their ability to tie up entire industries, including our own.

There is nothing in this bill which will prevent individual unions from adopting the "follow the leader" technique which they have employed so effectively in the steel industry.

There is nothing in the bill which would prevent individual unions from enforcing demands for common termination dates. In fact, this program already has been achieved to a considerable degree in many industries. Once common termination dates have been established, it would be a simple matter for the unions to tie up an entire industry, without being penalized for engaging in conspiracy in violation of the act.

There is nothing in the bill to effectively prevent the locals of a national labor organization from adopting common policies and objectives with respect to wage increases or working conditions.

There is nothing in this bill which would prevent a union from assisting another union financially, or by means of sympathetic boycotts or strikes. In other words, the bill would have little practical effect in curbing the economic power of labor unions.

On the other hand, the bill undoubtedly would weaken the relative position of employers in collective bargaining. We have learned from bitter experience in shipping and many other industries that effective employer organization is essential in order to keep a proper balance in the collective bargaining process. This bill apparently recognizes the advantages of group bargaining, for it permits group bargaining in a restricted area. We contend that the same benefits which accrue from the community-wide bargaining, which this bill permits, will result from group bargaining on an even larger area in the shipping industry.

The abrogation of our present contracts would mean the discontinuance of established machinery for voluntary arbitration and adjustment of grievances on a group or area basis. This would be a step backward. On the west coast, coastwide joint employer-employee committees have been established to handle grievances and to interpret the contract and working rules. A standing arbitrator has been appointed to adjudicate disputes which cannot be resolved by this joint committee. Under this system of area administration we are developing a uniformity of interpretation and precedents which tend to minimize the number of disputes and stoppages of work.

On the east coast various groups of employers negotiate jointly with the unions and sign individual but identical contracts. The provisions of this bill would preclude joint arbitration on an area-wide basis under these identical contracts.

Obviously, the advantages of any area system of joint administration and adjudication of grievances would be minimized if the coverage of our contracts were reduced to the local areas proposed in S. 133. A breakdown of our joint collective bargaining systems in shipping would vastly multiply the focal points for disputes arising not only out of negotiation of agreements, but also the day-by-day disputes on the job. The sum total of interruptions of service, on account of job action and "quickie" strikes is a matter of great concern to the public. It is in the public interest to continue and strengthen established mechanisms for adjudicating these day-by-day interruptions of commerce on as wide an area or group basis as possible. In the long run these disputes which tie up individual ships, individual piers and local ports, have proved more disastrous to shipping and to commerce than national tie-ups.

It has been argued that industry-wide bargaining will result in monopolistic price fixing through the collusion of large groups of employers and large unions. This objection to industry-wide bargaining has no possible application to ship-

ping. Domestic shipping rates are subject to control and regulation by the ICC. Rates on traffic by subsidized lines in the international trade are subject to the approval of the Maritime Commission. International shipping rates generally are fixed by keen competition among many maritime nations. It will thus be seen that it is impossible for the shipping industry to manipulate shipping rates through connivance with national maritime unions.

The proper remedy for monopolistic abuses by either unions or employers is to make them both equally subject to the antitrust laws rather than a ban on industry-wide bargaining.

Charles E. Wilson · GENERAL MOTORS CORPORATION

MY name is Charles E. Wilson and my home address is West Long Lake Road, Bloomfield Hills, Mich. I am president of General Motors Corp., having occupied that position since 1941. I have been associated with General Motors Corp. for over 27 years. During all of this time I have been close to factory operations and the day-to-day problems of employees. During the last 10 years I have devoted much of my time to employee relations particularly as they are affected by labor unions. . . .

When I appeared before your predecessor committee about a year ago, big strikes and threats of even bigger ones were interfering with the postwar prosperity of the Nation. It was a trying time for all. An effort was being made to find legislative solutions for our problems. The effort did not succeed. The strikes and difficulties were finally cleared up at

enormous cost to the country and considerable hardship to millions. I am sure that most citizens now see clearly that we must reform our labor laws and their administration so that the conditions we faced in 1946 with organized unemployment in the form of strikes and the resulting lack of production will not be repeated.

On account of large national and industry-wide strikes, and thousands of smaller ones as well, the country lost more than 100,000,000 tons of coal, almost 10,000,000 tons of finished steel, more than 1,500,000 cars and trucks, more than 100,000 homes, and substantial production of thousands of items.

In General Motors alone employees lost wages in excess of $200,000,000; the Government lost at least $60,000,000 in taxes; our customers went without more than 1,000,000 cars and trucks which

Reprinted from *Hearings before the Committee on Labor and Public Welfare,* Labor Relations Program, United States Senate, Eightieth Congress, First Session on S. 55 and S. J. Res. 22, Part I, pp. 473, 474–475, 484–485, 488–489, 472.

could have been produced. What the company, our material and parts suppliers, and our dealers lost is difficult to figure, but it was substantial. Very real losses for all by any standard?

I am very hopeful that the effort now being made will result in real progress toward labor peace. It is well to remember, however, that the sword of Damocles still hangs over our heads and will until our labor laws are fundamentally corrected.

In our mechanical age with its necessary and desirable mass production the problem of establishing sound industry-labor relations exists throughout the world. A real solution of the problem has not been worked out anywhere. Experiments are being tried in many countries on a tremendous scale which have forced revolutionary changes in governments themselves. It seems clear that none of these experiments which have eliminated free competition has been successful or that the people have gained. Free competition in labor, the right to compete for a job and earn a living, is just as important as free competition in business and industry. The country will really be prosperous and the people contented and happy when we stimulate the initiative of the millions and not the dictatorship of the few.

Many laws passed with good intentions to achieve desirable objectives not only fail to achieve those objectives but develop a whole new series of problems and abuses. Our current labor laws are in this class and need a real overhauling.

Many of our difficulties come from the fact that some of the ideas back of these laws or read into them were imported from abroad where conditions are different and the objectives of the people are not the same as they are in our country. Abroad, these same ideas ultimately developed either cartels and monopolistic unions or some form of state socialism or communism.

Americans do not like the end result that this foreign political economic philosophy has developed and is developing in Europe. At the very least it would be wise for Americans to observe how England develops and works out its current socialistic experiments before we commit ourselves irrevocably to a similar course. There certainly is a grave question as to whether England can achieve efficient production in its socialized industries without resorting to coercion and the destruction of personal freedom and, finally, the dictatorship which has been the result of such political philosophy in all other countries.

Last April one of the American delegates for industry who attended the Toledo meeting of the Metal Industries Section of the International Labor Office had the following experience:

Seventeen industrial countries were represented. The labor representative present urged that the ILO recommend industry-wide collective bargaining to the nations of the world. Employer representatives from foreign countries didn't advance any substantial objections.

In a closed session of employer representatives, this American delegate asked each of the 16 foreign delegates: "Can you fix prices and form cartels in your country, and does this have a bearing on your acceptance of industry-wide collective bargaining?"

They all said "yes."

What we need is a constructive American approach to the problem which will foster progress, promote free competition and preserve personal freedom and opportunity. This approach must at the same time recognize and preserve unions as proper organizations for group action by workmen. Likewise, it must establish practical and effective collective bargaining by free management and free unions with a minimum of damage to the people as a whole which might otherwise result from the abuse of the strike privilege. . . .

The monopoly power of national and international unions must be curbed by law. Industry-wide bargaining should be prohibited as it is the essence of monopoly in labor relations and if carried to its logical conclusion throughout all American industry will destroy our free competitive system. This monopoly power exercised through industry-wide bargaining has already challenged the supreme power of Government and, if sound corrective measures are not taken now, the power may develop to a point where some day such minority pressure group action will destroy our free society. Therefore, in principle I am in favor of any legislation which would effectively prohibit industry-wide bargaining. There are various possible ways of accomplishing the same purpose, other than those in the proposed legislation, which should be explored. One possible way would be to withdraw the sanction of law for collective bargaining by unions having or exercising monopoly power.

Americans do not like monopolies or dictators of any kind. They do not like them in Government and politics, in finance and industry, and it is becoming increasingly clear that they do not like them in labor either. Americans instinctively fear the loss of individual liberty through the abuse of power that a monopoly or any form of dictatorship creates.

The present industrial unions are the most powerful monopolies that have ever existed. They threaten the economic security of the Nation. Those who think they have vested interests in monopolies do not give them up easily. Many reasons, some of them plausible on their face, have and will be advanced for perpetuating this present unrestricted power. In this, unions may be joined by individual employers and groups of employers who are a part of a monopolistic industry control established by industry-wide bargaining, because of the manner in which their industry monopoly controls restrict competition.

Senate 133 provides one way of decreasing and limiting this labor monopoly power. I am in favor of this legislation unless some more effective and practical method is found to accomplish the same purpose. I have thought of two others that might be considered: First, using the same principles as stated in S. 133, but instead of confining the monopoly power to areas, confine it to States. The advantages of such a provision would be that the States have established boundaries and fundamentally the power to deal with this problem within their own borders. This would get around the difficulty of defining labor areas.

Another way for accomplishing this purpose would be to restrict the designation of employee representatives to labor organizations whose jurisdiction in this regard would be limited to employees of one employer. This would not prohibit such organizations from maintaining affiliations with other labor organizations representing employees of other employers, but would simply require that they act autonomously in all of their own affairs and not be subject to control by representatives of employees of other employers or by national or international officers of the organization with which they may be affiliated.

In order to implement this policy further, it is also proposed that the laws be amended to provide that any agreement that represents an illegal restraint of trade when entered into between two employers shall also be illegal if entered into by an employer and a labor organization or by the representatives of the employees of two or more employers. Controversies covering such matters should not constitute labor disputes within the meaning of the Norris-LaGuardia Act, and the penalties provided by the Clayton and Sherman Acts for such conduct should be equally applicable to labor organizations engaging in them by agreement with employers.

This would place the national unions in about the same relationship to their locals as national trade associations are with respect to their employer members. . . .

The privilege of striking has been recognized as proper action for employees to take when they consider that as a group they are being exploited or are not receiving fair treatment in regard to wages, hours, and working conditions.

It was never intended that this privilege should be used as a means of aggression against all other citizens. It is comparable to the basic right that all nations have to defend themselves against aggression, as compared to the development of a military machine for the purpose of aggression against other nations.

General strikes or national strikes affecting the health and safety of the people or the economic security of great numbers of citizens not directly involved in the dispute immediately become a challenge to government, which has the responsibility of maintaining law and order and protecting the interests of all citizens. Our labor laws and the legislative and judicial procedures to be followed must be clarified so that a situation like that which developed in the recent coal strike would not have to be resolved by the chance technical maneuver of accusing a labor leader of being in contempt of court. Clearly no pressure group can be allowed to challenge the supreme power of government. The legal procedure through which this power of government is to be exercised must be clearly defined and understood by all.

Americans have respect for their courts. They know that the courts are the safeguard of their individual liberties. The privilege of striking cannot be carried to the point where general strikes or industry-wide strikes cripple the economy of the Nation. It is important to distinguish this type of strike. When the public interest is involved in a vital manner, it should be clearly understood that courts have the unquestioned rights to restrain those instigating and participating in strikes of this type. If the privileges of unions are clearly defined by law in this regard, few would be so bold or so irresponsible as to call such strikes even though they might have the monopoly power to do so.

The responsibility for applying the law has historically resided in our courts. The enforcement of the decrees of courts is the responsibility of the administrative branch of government. When this authority of the courts is challenged, the responsibility for the enforcement of their decrees rests upon the administrative branches of government — Federal, State, and local. If the procedures are established by law and clearly understood beforehand, the enforcement powers of government will rarely, if ever, have to be invoked.

Certain of the bills before the committee — namely S. 55, S. 130, S. 360, and S. 404 — recognize this problem and attempt to deal with it in part, by restricting the monopoly power of unions in various ways and eliminating legal immunities which strikers enjoy under present law. However, none of this proposed legislation deals directly with the issue of the abuse of the privilege of striking when carried to this extreme. Other and more effective legislation than that which has been proposed will be required. . . .

SENATOR SMITH. Then you would suggest that in the case of national paralysis the court should have injunctive power to restrain a strike?

MR. WILSON. I certainly do.

SENATOR SMITH. And say to a man, "You must go back to work"? How are you going to force them to go back, if there are 400,000 of them, as there were in the coal strike?

MR. WILSON. If they think to go back to work is the right thing to do and it is clearly described as a part of our process, the men are not going to continue such a strike. The reason they strike in cases like this is because they think they have that right. You cannot say that the Government, finally, has not the supreme power.

C. Dickerman Williams · AMERICAN LOCOMOTIVE
COMPANY

MR. WILLIAMS. Mr. Chairman and gentlemen, my name is C. Dickerman Williams. I am vice president and general counsel of American Locomotive Co., 30 Church Street, New York, N. Y.

American Locomotive Co. manufactures steam and Diesel locomotives at its plant at Schenectady, N. Y.; Diesel engines at Auburn, N. Y.; pressure vessels, tubular equipment, heat transfer equipment and the like at Dunkirk, N. Y.; and steel springs and tires for railway use at Latrobe, Pa. At the present time it employs at those plants approximately 11,500 men and women. Its plants at Schenectady, Auburn, Dunkirk, and Latrobe are all organized by the United Steel Workers of America [USWA], CIO. . . .

The company has other plants in the United States and its subsidiary has a plant in Canada.

This statement is confined to the company's relations with USWA at its plants

at Schenectady, Auburn, Dunkirk, and Latrobe, and particularly to its plant at Schenectady, which is by far the largest plant of the company.

American Locomotive Co.'s collective bargaining agreements are all with the USWA International. This is in accordance with article XVII of the steel workers' constitution, which provides that the international union shall be a party to all collective bargaining agreements, and all such agreements shall be signed by the international officers. . . .

I am here in support of S. 113, the bill introduced by Senator Ball to forbid industry-wide bargaining on a national basis. The bill permits company bargaining, permits industry-wide bargaining on a local basis, which meets our objection to bargaining on a national basis. . . .

There is no doubt that all our contracts are controlled by Steel Workers International at Pittsburgh, but the contracts themselves are separate. That was

Reprinted from *Hearings before the Committee on Labor and Public Welfare*, Labor Relations Program, United States Senate, Eightieth Congress, First Session on S. 55 and S. J. Res. 22, Part I, pp. 206–207, 208–211, 215–217, 220–222.

brought out very sharply in the strike of 1946 where, although we negotiated, we had one set of negotiations at Schenectady, another set at Auburn, another set at Dunkirk; but it was perfectly clear that the centralized power at Pittsburgh was sitting in and controlling; in fact, they made no secret about it that they were controlling the progress of those negotiations insofar as the locals were concerned. . . .

SENATOR ELLENDER. You spoke of the international representative having a veto power. To what extent does he exercise it over the views of the workers, who are really the ones that are interested, or should be interested, in any collective bargaining?

MR. WILLIAMS. If the local seems to be willing to make a contract that does not fit in with the wishes of the international, their representative simply vetoes it.

SENATOR ELLENDER. Who are the sufferers under that plan, as a rule, the local workers?

MR. WILLIAMS. I think we are all sufferers. The American Locomotive Co. and the employees are both sufferers. In other words, we can't get together with our own employees and bargain collectively, because if we want to do something that happens to suit us —

SENATOR ELLENDER (interposing). And the employees?

MR. WILLIAMS. And the employees, yes, — but that does not suit the international because they regard it as an undesirable precedent, we can't make the contract.

SENATOR ELLENDER. Can you be a little more specific on that?

MR. WILLIAMS. Yes, I am going to be. I am going to describe an outstanding illustration of the way we were controlled last winter. . . . The reason for our support of S. 133 is that our recent experience indicates that the company cannot have collective bargaining with its employees when all agreements must be ratified and approved by the international.

The strike of 1946 at the plants of the American Locomotive Co. would never have taken place if the local unions had been permitted to proceed by collective bargaining, as distinguished from the exercise of centralized power by the international.

Industry-wide bargaining gives little encouragement to the individual employer to establish favorable labor relations.

Even a medium-sized employer, like ourselves, is at a great disadvantage in dealing with a centralized union of 800,000 members, such as the steel workers.

Industry-wide bargaining gives no recognition to the widely varying economic and social factors applicable to the employers of the various union members, and of the localities in which they reside.

The American Locomotive Co. believes that the enactment of S. 133, by requiring collective bargaining on a company or local level, will strongly tend to remedy this situation, and the company therefore supports S. 133.

I should like to summarize our experience in support of this conclusion.

I first want to give the background of our company's labor situation immediately preceding the strike of 1946.

In the winter of 1945–46 our company held large orders for steam locomotives for devastated European countries, particularly France. These orders had been substantially financed by the United States Government to speed European rehabilitation. The company was also at that time just putting into production a Diesel electric road locomotive of a new and improved design. It was exceedingly important to the company that the work on the new Diesel electric road locomotive proceed as rapidly and vigorously as possible because of the intense competition in this field and because the use of the company's facilities for armament manufacture during the war had handicapped it in the maintenance of its competitive position.

The locomotive industry, and particularly American Locomotive, pays high wages. According to a release by the Bureau of Labor Statistics issued February 21, 1946, the locomotive industry had paid in December, 1945, average weekly earnings of $60.92, and average hourly earnings of $1.398. This was in contrast with weekly earnings of $41.43, as stated in the same release, for all manufacturing in that month, and hourly earnings of $0.997. The average wages paid by American Locomotive Co. at Schenectady were somewhat higher than that reported by the Bureau of Labor Statistics for the locomotive industry as a whole. I therefore think it is fair to say that we are one of the highest wage payers in the United States.

. . . Until the strike of January, 1946, the company had not had any serious strikes in 20 years.

In the latter part of 1945 the Steel Workers International published a demand for an additional $2 a day or 25 cents an hour on all collective-bargaining agreements coming up for renewal, and shortly thereafter a demand for this amount was presented to the company by all our steel workers locals. It soon developed that the local officials had no authority to reduce this figure; in short, had no authority to bargain. We pointed to the high wages which we paid, to the efforts that we had made in maintaining friendly labor relations, to the fact that the wages of the piecework employees were steadily increasing as time went on because, through greater familiarity with the art, with their task, the pieceworkers were able to earn larger sums.

The only answer the local officers could make to these arguments was that the instructions from the international did not permit any deviation from the $2 a day demand.

Then the Steel Workers International announced a strike would be called on January 14, 1946, if no settlement had been achieved by that date. This announcement, I think, was made December 11, 1945. This strike call applied to all members of the Steel Workers, including the employees of over 1,100 steel fabricators, like American Locomotive Co. However, the call was made dependent upon negotiations with a single employer, the United States Steel Corp., and that employer was not a fabricator of steel products, like ourselves, but was a producer of steel; in other words, not really in the same industry that we are.

Perhaps it would be helpful if I went outside this statement — SENATOR ELLENDER (interposing). But you are entirely dependent on the United States Steel Corp. for steel, are you not?

MR. WILLIAMS. That and other steel producers. In fact, as I am going on later to explain, the steel producers got this $5 a ton increase, but they took it out of us. No price relief was given to us. In fact, we really could not get it because we had long-term contracts at fixed prices.

I think it would be helpful if I went outside this brief to explain briefly the type of employer that is organized by the Steel Workers International. The Steel Workers International, I understand, has approximately 800,000 members, of whom a little more than half are employed by steel producers, such as United States Steel, Bethlehem Steel, and so on. The remaining somewhat less than 50 percent are employed by a very large number of steel fabricators such as ourselves; that is to say, users and buyers of steel, people who make steel products which are widely diversified and generally not competitive with each other. We make railway equipment. The steel workers have organized other railway equipment manufacturers, but they have also organized manufacturers of cutlery, hardware, machinery, and equipment generally. In fact, I have been told that they have organized Van Camp's Pork and Beans, showing how widely scattered the employees are. But for the most part the employers organized by the Steel Workers International are users of steel, fabricators of steel.

These one-thousand-one-hundred-odd fabricators are, of course, scattered throughout the country. Most of them are relatively small manufacturers, relatively to the great steel producers, and their competitors are not necessarily organized by Steel Workers. For instance, in the locomotive field one of our principal competitors is organized by the Steel Workers and another by the UAW, and particularly at our plant at Dunkirk, which manufactures tubular equipment, the competitors, most of them, are not organized by the Steel Workers. Some of them are, but I should say the majority were not. That was one reason why the strike was particularly severe on our Dunkirk plant, because most of the rest of the industry went steadily ahead during this period without strikes, and we took every bad loss in the competitive position for that reason. . . .

The results of the strike were several. The company had suffered a severe setback. Equipment vital to domestic and European recovery had been long delayed. The employees went without wages for from 2 to 3 months. Moreover, this wage increase and the blow suffered by the national economy from the absence of production during this period precipitated a wave of price increases which more than swallowed up the benefits of the 18½ cents, particularly with such highly paid employees, to whom 18½ cents was a relatively small proportion. In terms of real wages for 1946 the employee had a substantial loss.

We could, as a result of this experience, conclude only that we had been engaged in something new in American employee-employer relationship. We had engaged, not even in industry-wide bargaining, but in a new thing which might be called "industries-wide bargaining." This was a type of bargaining which lumped indiscriminately all companies making or using the same commodity, regardless of their economic or competitive position, or the locality in which they carried on their operations.

Because we believe that situations such as have been described are a threat both to the process of true collective bargaining and to freely competitive industry, American Locomotive Co. records its support of S. 133, forbidding industry-wide bargaining on a national basis.

I might emphasize that we are not opposed to collective bargaining. We are fully satisfied to bargain with our own employees, who, after all, realize that the welfare of the company is a factor. What we do not want is to bargain with a vast, remote institution of whom our employees constitute only a negligible fraction, and who are not concerned with the welfare of the company, to whom the welfare of the company is of no substantial account, and who are more concerned with establishing precedents or avoiding precedents that might affect negotiations carried on elsewhere, on operations affecting the wages of the entire 800,000 group.

THE CHAIRMAN. Mr. Williams, as I see it, if this bill were enacted, your six local unions to which you refer, and maybe other unions, could then associate themselves in a joint association of some sort. I assume, even in spite of this bill, that association could negotiate with you for all the four plants?

MR. WILLIAMS. I so construe the bill.

THE CHAIRMAN. You would have no objection to such an association of unions?

MR. WILLIAMS. No, sir.

THE CHAIRMAN. You are not trying necessarily to set up plant unions in each plant?

MR. WILLIAMS. No, we are satisfied with this bill.

THE CHAIRMAN. How effective do you think a law of that sort would be? How effective do you think, even if that set-up were made and the international union were forbidden to be a party to the contract or to order things, do you think that by general association your unions would still make the same demands as the other unions in the United Steel Workers?

MR. WILLIAMS. I suppose it is a speculation, but in my opinion the bill would be effective. I think that if the employees had independence of action, we would have true collective bargaining with our employees. I think the controlling factor

is not necessarily some such clause as article XVII in the Steel Workers constitution, which requires that the International be a party to all collective-bargaining agreements, but membership in the International as such; because, after all, if the individual members of the local remain members of the International, and the locals as subject to centralized control as they are by the Steel Workers constitution, even in the absence of such a clause as article XVII, the International could effect control over the local.

THE CHAIRMAN. I am just wondering whether you can effectively stop that control. That has been my principal question on this attempt to stop industry-wide bargaining, whether it would be an effective thing, although the association, voluntary association of different unions may not continue so that the International has a man, so to speak, in your union and in some other union —

MR. WILLIAMS (interposing). I don't think they would permit it.

THE CHAIRMAN. You don't think the American Locomotive unions would permit such domination indirectly?

MR. WILLIAMS. It might take a little time to develop new habits of thinking, but if they had freedom of action I think they would exercise it, because conditions vary so. I think that this bill does not prevent affiliation, or would not prevent some kind of affiliation.

THE CHAIRMAN. If there should be such affiliation, then I wonder if that would not work out in pretty much the same kind of control as you have today?

MR. WILLIAMS. I don't think so. I think conditions are so different that if our locals had freedom of action they would exercise it. It might take a little time before they realized that they could think and act for themselves, but I think that would soon take place, and there would be a great difference in conditions.

SENATOR BALL. You say you were closed down an additional week or two because, after the local had negotiated a contract with you and signed it, the International vetoed it?

MR. WILLIAMS. That is right. Our men never would have struck last winter if it had not been for the fear of this industry-wide thing. They were making good money and were satisfied to continue. . . .

SENATOR ELLENDER. Mr. Williams, you stated a while ago that your employees were perfectly satisfied, and that probably if they had been permitted to go along you could have contracted with them. Suppose the 18½ cents increase had been allowed to other segments of labor, do you think your people would have been satisfied to maintain the same rates that were prevailing just before this increase was given?

MR. WILLIAMS. That is a pretty speculative question. At that time we did not know that the general price increase would take place. I think that if we alone had been outside the national pattern, if we for some reason or other had had just a union company-wide and all these other increases took place and the economy was prostrated, as it was, and then the other increases went on, price increases went on, we would have made some kind of adjustment. . . .

SENATOR PEPPER. Suppose that there is a competitor of yours engaged in the same business. Suppose your employees are organized and have a strong union and thereby force a good wage scale out of you. But suppose your competitor has a group of employees who are not organized or it is not a strong union, and he can force a lower wage scale out of his workers than you are able to get. Would

that not give him an advantage in the market in competition with you, based upon the cheaper labor cost?

MR. WILLIAMS. Oh, no; you have to pay good wages to get good work. I believe in collective bargaining. Do not think that I am opposed to collective bargaining. I claim we do not get collective bargaining.

SENATOR PEPPER. I say then there is an arguable advantage and fairness about the wage scale throughout an industry being comparable and relative, is there not?

MR. WILLIAMS. I would say that it failed to reflect local conditions. I think in a given area where the same living costs apply to all the workers, what you say is true. And as I understand, that is recognized by Senator Ball's bill.

SENATOR PEPPER. Yes. But if you and your competitor have comparable characteristics about your industry, if you have relatively the same number in rural areas, and so forth, is it not desirable that you and he be able to compete at a market at about the same labor-cost basis, as far as human labor is concerned? And is it not better for you not to have that fellow undersell you in the market because he is able to exact lower-paid work out of his workers than you are?

MR. WILLIAMS. Senator Pepper, I do not think your hypothesis applies to our industry. You seem to be assuming that if our competitor can get as good work out of his employees at lower wages from us, he will have a certain advantage. Well, that would apply only, in the first place, if he were in a place where other factors were equal, such as freight rates and supply of labor, and so forth.

Even at that, if we say the freight rates are equal, the supply of labor is equal, and all the other factors are equal, and at the same time for some other reason he is able to get lower wages and as much work out of his employees as we can, that is simply — that is obvious. But that does not apply to our industry.

SENATOR PEPPER. All right.

MR. WILLIAMS. Furthermore, I would like to make this point, Senator Pepper, with respect to the Steel Workers, that the Steel Workers have organized a lot of industries. The Steel Workers are scat-

tered around. Not all the locomotive manufacturers are organized by the Steel Workers, as I pointed out in one part of my statement. One locomotive manufacturer, organized by a different union, went right through this strike without any cessation of work and gained that advantage not because it paid higher wages or because it had better labor relations but simply because it had a different union.

Hugh H. C. Weed · CARTER CARBURETOR CORPORATION

... BECAUSE I wish to approach this subject on the basis of fundamentals, I have listed as the first reason to prohibit industry, the effect it has on the individual. Again it seems uppermost that the individual's freedom to work and freedom of association must prevail.

In virtually every plant that has a union any employee in the local has access to the representatives or officers of the local union. He can attend meetings of the local union and express his views to his fellow workers and to his bargaining representatives on matters of importance to him in his work.

The individual is an individual in his local union. The problems, interests, and living conditions are mutual to him and his fellow workers. In bargaining he understands the conditions he is bargaining about.

In one company in which I am a stockholder they tell me that the interests and desires of employees performing similar types of work in widely scattered plants engaged in the manufacture of similar products vary greatly. In three different plants of this company, the employees

wanted and obtained vastly different seniority provisions in their contract. One provides for plant-wide seniority, another for departmental seniority and a third for job seniority. The employees of one plant owned by a subsidiary of this company have requested and have been granted a holiday on the "first day of small game season." This plant is located in a rural area. The employees at this plant preferred this holiday because of local interests. No such request has been made at other plants of this company.

The employees of this company in one plant negotiated time and one-half on Saturday as such except in weeks in which holidays occur, when Saturday is considered a regular work day and paid for at straight time. Other contracts of this company require time and one-half on Saturday whether or not a holiday falls within the workweek. These provisions directly opposed to one another arise because the plant permitting work on Saturday at straight time is located in a small community where the employees desire at least 5 days' work every week. Employees in other communities, princi-

From hearings on S. 55 and S. J. Res. 22, United States Senate, Committee on Labor and Public Welfare, 80th Congress, 1st Session, part 2, February 1947, pp. 908–910.

pally metropolitan areas seem to prefer to sacrifice a day's pay rather than work on Saturday.

Thus the interests and wishes of employees in different localities vary considerably. So long as collective bargaining is conducted on a local basis, these employees obtain terms of employment of their own choosing. It keeps the relationship human, intimate, soluble.

Industry-wide bargaining compels employees to accept conditions not in accord with their wishes and makes the relationship distant, rigid, and much less soluble.

Far more important, it destroys the freedom of the employee in a local plant. He has little voice in, and virtually no opportunity to express his personal views on, the terms of a labor agreement under which he must work. His freedom is gone.

Secondly, industry-wide bargaining tends to destroy the economic security of many rural areas. There now exists in many small communities one establishment of a large company. Such local industries create concentration of inhabitants more or less proportionate to the employment needs of the rural plant. The rural plant supports these small communities, the local bank, stores, and transportation companies.

Certain basic costs are greater in these rural plants. A substantial one is inbound and out-bound freight. For example, take any heavy commodity made of steel. The cost of transporting steel which constitutes most of its material is from certain basing points. In some metropolitan areas, the freight is relatively nominal — say 5 cents per 100 pounds — whereas in rural areas it may run as high as 34 cents per 100 pounds. Thus rural plants must pay substantial additional cost in delivered raw material.

But the cost of living there is less which justifies a differential in wages.

Now comes industry-wide bargaining demanding that the historical differential in wages be abolished. The rural plant cannot continue under such circumstances, thus throwing men out of work and disrupting the economic security of such rural communities.

Thirdly, industry-wide bargaining tends to eliminate small business. The small business generally lacks the working capital or mechanical equipment of many larger industries. On the other hand it frequently offers more rapid advancement to the employees than large business does, and a better opportunity to learn the business. These advantages justify a lower base wage which is accepted by employees for the above reasons. The same small business frequently adopts a type of incentive plan which produces even greater earnings for its employees in spite of a lower base rate. Industry-wide bargaining destroys this opportunity for high earnings through special incentives when it forces the industry-wide pattern upon the small business.

Fourthly, industry-wide bargaining may impair our national defense. We have heard a great deal recently about decentralizing industry to scatter the risk in case of attack with modern weapons of war. For the reasons outlined above, industry-wide bargaining, by tending to eliminate rural plants and the opportunity of small business to survive, in effect drives industry into metropolitan areas. This is directly opposed to the desired decentralization of industries.

Fifthly, and most important, industry-wide bargaining has created monopoly and excessive power in the hands of a few national labor leaders. Experience with the huge unions in the past year virtually makes my point a truism requiring little argument. We have seen national union leaders endeavoring to deliver the vote of the union membership in political campaigns. One man was able to completely shut off one of the principal supplies of fuel endangering our industrial and economic structure and the very health and lives of the people. This would be impossible without industry-wide bargaining. Consider the terrible consequences that would flow from an industry-wide shutdown of power or of cutting off other types of services or commodities on which large segments of the population depend.

There is no greater peril to the workers themselves as well as the general public than industry-wide bargaining. We recommend that this Congress adopt legislation which will effectively prohibit the continuation or enlargement of this practice. . . .

Twentieth Century Fund:

LABOR AND MANAGEMENT LOOK AT COLLECTIVE BARGAINING

A Canvass of Leaders' Views

UNION leaders are divided in opinion on the advantages of different types of bargaining units. Some few prefer single-plant or single-company bargaining. Three out of four choose multi-employer contracts. Among those that prefer to bargain with a group of employers, half think of local or regional contracts, half of nation-wide contracts.

Among business executives, likewise, all nuances of opinion are represented, but the proponents of nation-wide bargaining are outnumbered by opponents of this method of negotiation.

Both parties favor bargaining units somewhat larger than at present. Among the union leaders, multi-company bargaining is twice as popular as single-company or single-plant negotiation. Businessmen lean almost as much the other way.

PREFERENCES OF UNION LEADERS

Most national union leaders are striving for larger bargaining units, fewer contracts and greater uniformity of wages and working conditions. . . . Preference for single-plant bargaining was voiced by only 4 of the 49 union leaders who answered the question, "If you had your choice, which type of coverage would you choose (single-plant or employer, employers in a limited area or a large part of an entire industry) for your union's agreements?" Nine labor leaders

Selected excerpts from *Labor and Management Look at Collective Bargaining* by W. S. Woytinsky. Twentieth Century Fund, 1949. Reprinted by permission.

would choose to deal with one employer at a time, but not plant by plant. Nine others gave no preference, which usually meant that individual plant negotiation was acceptable to them. . . .

The reason given most often for preferring group bargaining was that it reduces the danger of competitive wage-cutting and ensures uniformity in wage patterns. The preference for dealing with groups of employers does not extend, however, to industry-wide negotiation. Of the 45 union leaders who discussed this question, 19 (representing 47 per cent of the total union membership) favored industry-wide negotiation and 20 opposed it. . . . Thirteen opposed nationwide contracts in view of the differences in local conditions. Even among those who want industry-wide bargaining, several regard it as an indefinite future hope rather than an immediate goal.

Single-Plant Bargaining

The labor officials who expressed a preference for single-plant negotiations gave as their reason the tactical advantage of dealing with smaller, and presumably weaker, employer units. Some, however, were not very sure that this method of collective bargaining is the most effective.

We always confine our agreements to one plant. We think this is guerrilla war. Advance where you can, retreat where you must — but don't allow them to get you lined up on one long front. We want to keep employers apart. And if we can continue to do that, the Taft-Hartley law is going to be worth 10 cents an hour to every worker. You know, hope deferred makes the heart sick, but strikes deferred make it pretty useless for employers to plan. And so they're soon in the hope-deferred class — and then they give us what we want and we give them what they want, and everybody's happy.

I believe the company-wide agreement is better but it is still in the experimental stage. So at least for the present, I prefer the single-plant agreement. . . .

Single-Company Bargaining

The union officials who said they preferred single-company bargaining considered the company, instead of the plant, to be the logical basic unit of negotiation. Some of them were giving thought to the question of larger units of bargaining but were not pressing for a change.

We deal mostly with individual companies. We might go for an area rather than a national set-up, perhaps like New England. But the operations of a lot of companies are very different. However, we'd like health and other benefits comparable all over the country.

* * *

All our contracts are with single employers. We have a few instances where we negotiate jointly, but even then we write separate contracts with each employer. We have one master agreement which covers a chain of plants on basic issues but leaves the determination of details for local bargaining. I could think only in city-wide terms. There aren't any associations which could represent employers beyond a single community, and we haven't particularly sought even that. . . .

Bargaining with Employer Associations

Uniformity was the keynote struck by the union leaders who prefer to bargain with local employer associations. Area agreements, they said, not only establish uniformity of wage rates but also help to maintain uniform working conditions and standards of work. No company is penalized for dealing with the union, and all the workers get the same benefits from collective bargaining. Another advantage mentioned was more orderly negotiations.

We have roughly 90 collective agreements and 900 independent agreements. Dealing with an association simplifies a lot of problems for employers and for unions. We definitely prefer dealing with groups of employers. You establish uniformity of standards in the area. You eliminate disparities of standards between firms. You even eliminate causing a disadvantage to a firm which may be willing to deal with a union. Also you can discuss the general pattern or relationships on a much sounder basis. You can establish permanent arbitration machinery, build up experienced negotiators. In this way you can be fair to both sides and to the public. with independent contracts, the individual employer can't support a permanent arbitrator. . . .

Industry-wide Bargaining

About as many union leaders oppose industry-wide bargaining as favor it. . . . It appears, however, that those who advocate centralized negotiation are more insistent than those who oppose it.

In the industries where bargaining is centralized, the union officials regard nation-wide contracts as essential, and several others consider such a system of bargaining as a leading objective.

Industry-wide agreement is necessary in our field because of the competitive situation. If you stabilize the wage bill in the industry as a whole, you remove the incentive for operators to reduce wages for competitive purposes.

*   *   *

We're trying to get all our workers under one agreement for the industry. The employers have found this better. We believe an industry agreement is better than individual agreements. Under individual agreements, you always go after your friends first, and that puts them at a disadvantage. . . .

The attitude of opponents of industry-wide bargaining is skeptical rather than antagonistic. Most of them simply do not believe this method would work in their particular industry.

I'm in favor of the idea of nation-wide bargaining, but I don't think it is too practical in our industry because of the different nature of the work and the different kinds of work they have to handle.

*   *   *

We would like industry bargaining, but in our industry it's rather difficult to do because of living costs, which differ between, say, New York and small towns. Also, the employers sell to local markets. A small plant in a small town has to send its trucks many miles; in New York, trucks can deliver all the output in a small area. . . .

Variable Bargaining Patterns

The statements of union leaders that they have no preference for any particular type of agreement indicate that they desire to use whatever method of bargaining best fits the particular circumstances. As one of the interviewed union leaders put it, they decide each case on its merits. However, some unions that use various types of bargaining are trying to shape their contracts into one or two preferred patterns.

We couldn't state any preference. Each case is decided on its own merits, and we'll accept any type of contract which will mean most benefits for our members. . . .

PREFERENCES OF BUSINESS EXECUTIVES

The business executives were asked: "How does your company negotiate wage contracts — by itself alone, or jointly with some or all of the firms in your industry? Which way is best?" In replying, all but a few approved of the arrangement they had. Some local trade and service firms, however, indicated a desire to change from individual negotiation to group negotiation, and a few railroad men complained about the restrictions of the national conference procedure, of which other rail officials spoke approvingly.

Independent dealing by the single company is liked best by two thirds of the manufacturing companies and one third of the nonmanufacturing firms. . . . Local group bargaining is preferred by executives of 16 nonmanufacturing and 8 manufacturing companies. The method favored depends essentially on the structure of the industry. The few firms which prefer industry-wide bargaining are mainly local or railroad companies. Several executives declared that their preference would depend on the circumstances of the bargaining.

Single-Company Bargaining

The reason given most often by business executives who chose single-company dealing was that each company's problems require special consideration.

We stand on our own feet and handle our own problems and that is the best way, we think. We have enough trouble correlating the problem in 25 plants throughout the country without taking on the problems of other companies.

* * *

We work alone, always have, and hope we always will. You know your own business and you deal for your own business. Of course that's best. . . .

In a few cases, the preference was not merely to have a company stand alone, but also to have independent negotiation by subsidiaries, company divisions or even individual plants. . . .

We make our own contracts and they are not even company-wide; they deal with each

particular plant separately. That is the best way for us to handle negotiations; in fact, I think it's the only way.

Some businessmen condemned group bargaining.

We do not believe in any industry-wide bargaining. We think individual bargaining is best because any other leads to price fixing, to cartelization, to restriction of production. That would be the end of the free-enterprise system. All one has to do is to look at the coal industry to see what happens when there is industry-wide bargaining. . . .

A considerable number of the executives favor individual negotiation because they believe this method emphasizes the "human touch" in labor relations. They declared that better morale and more cordial relationships with the employee representatives result, and even that the employees get a better deal. . . .

We make our bargaining alone, that is the best way. We have been criticized because we're tarred with the accusation of being a leader, and in the light of that criticism we should deal by ourselves. Also, we find in that way we get more familiar and develop more intimate personal relations with the union officials, which enables us to understand one another better. . . .

The businessmen pointed out occasionally that individual bargaining may be strongly influenced by leadership which sets the pattern for the industry.

We do bargaining individually, but it has the effect of industry-wide negotiations. The union we deal with also deals with all the other producers. They negotiate with the small companies first. They might suggest that they settle for a 10-cents-an-hour increase with a reopening clause when the larger companies have settled. That is how they take care of the little fellow. The next step is to tackle us — we are big — and at the same time they negotiate with the other two major companies. It was obvious in the last negotiations that the others were held up for our settlement. One of the conciliators even suggested to the small companies that they settle for X cents an hour waiting for our settlement. We are fast approaching a pattern of industry-wide bargaining whether we call it that or not. However, in our American system the individual method is best. . . .

A number of executives, while preferring single-company bargaining for their own organization, recognized advantages in joint dealings by some others.

We do it all by ourselves. At one time, I thought it would be better if we could bargain on an industry-wide basis, but I know now that would never work. The local conditions will bar that. We'll bid against other employers, and we'll go along as best we can. That's the best way in our business. . . .

Local Group Bargaining

In local service industries and in manufacturing concerns with a chain of local plants, business executives prefer often to bargain with labor unions through an employer association or area wage committee.

A few of the business executives thought that negotiations could be handled best by informal wage committees representing a group of employers. More often, however, preference was given to a permanent organization with a specialized staff and years of experience.

We have contracts in 69 cities, and in not 5 per cent of the cases do we negotiate alone. We are in with the local firms in the area in virtually every case. This is sometimes more or less informal — a local committee comes together to deal with the unions as the occasion arises. Recently, however, I have been urging more formal employer associations.

It's better to have a more or less permanent organization with a hired staff to do the leg work. This is just formalizing and better organizing the informal committees. . . .

In a few industries in which the association method of bargaining is known to be well accepted, the interviewers sought the views of association officials to supplement those of company executives. Among the points made by the spokesmen of associations were that this method of bargaining is more orderly and keeps disputes to a minimum, that it gives the employers greater strength, that it reduces wage competition and that it gives the small employer a better break.

This is an employer association office and we negotiate on behalf of our members. It is better to negotiate jointly. Where there is good faith on the part of those who join together, it provides a way to get better results from negotiations. After all, these men all employ the same workers. And under this joint-negotiation idea, no one manufacturer can hope for a better return than the others. It's logical. . . .

Executives in local trade and in service industries and the utilities expressed a strong desire to change their method of bargaining, shifting from individual contracts to contracts established through employer associations. The common reasons for such a change were to remove wages from competition and to prevent the unions from playing one company off against another.

We negotiate alone, but that is not the best way for this industry. Retail trade is a highly competitive field. It is one of the few fields in which you do business in the same labor market and the same competitive market as your competitors. Next to the cost of merchandise, wages are our greatest item of cost. If one store can maintain a lower labor cost than the others, it has a tremendous competitive advantage. Collective dealing by all the stores on wages would take the wage advantage out of the area of competition and leave the stores to compete on a basis of managerial efficiency, service to the public and so on. The economic strength of one store in bargaining is pretty weak, whereas the strength of all the stores together would be pretty strong. . . .

Industry-wide Bargaining

The great majority of the businessmen interviewed oppose industry-wide bargaining. The few persons who favor it spoke for one of three industries: clothing, coal or railroads. Even in these fields, however, industry-wide negotiation was not favored unanimously.

The reason heard most often for preferring industry-wide dealing was that it prevents competitive overbidding and cutting of wages. Occasionally a reference was also made to equality for small business.

I really am in favor of national wage negotiations. From a competitive viewpoint, it puts all operators on the same footing. Then their reductions in costs can be made individually by mechanization and more efficient operation. In other words, one operator cannot undercut prices by exploiting labor.

* * *

Personally, I favor national negotiation. I think that, over the years, the industry will be as strong as the union. History leads me to believe that the economic health of the coal industry requires a strong union. We had an unhappy experience in the years after the Jacksonville agreement. When one company resigns, goes nonunion, starts cutting prices, then it begins neglecting safety.

The first thing you know, you have a situation that's bad for the industry. We in the coal industry are dependent on a strong union for a strong and coherent industry. . . .

Variable Bargaining Patterns

Many of the firms canvassed have both group and individual bargaining. As a rule, their executives were satisfied with the arrangements. They tended to stress the fact that the size of the bargaining unit should be adapted both to the structure of the industry and to the scope of the question to be negotiated.

We work both ways. With nine of the craft unions, we work in joint negotiation through the association. With the other unions, we have direct negotiations. Businesswise, the association handling of negotiations is much the better way. But it isn't feasible to handle all our problems in that way at this time.

* * *

The way we do it is generally determined by whether the issue is nation-wide or limited to one area. Some issues should be settled nationally, some locally.

A few of the management men who failed to express a definite preference felt that the union dictates the bargaining-unit pattern and therefore it is futile to consider a change.

I don't think you can really say which is best. It all depends on the circumstances. In some areas, manufacturers are on the labor committees of the associations, and in some areas, it's an all-out fight with one or two of the members who hold out. About all you could say is that in our industry, with the unions as strong as they are, it's a "must" to negotiate jointly. . . .

Suggestions for Additional Reading

An excellent brief introduction to the development of collective bargaining in the United States is found in the Twentieth Century Fund Report: S. T. Williamson and Herbert Harris, *Trends in Collective Bargaining* (New York, 1945), chapters 1–3. Collective bargaining policies and the relationship of the government to collective bargaining are well treated in Joseph Shister, *Economics of the Labor Market* (Chicago, 1949), chapters 7, 8, 9, 10, and 12.

For background on the history of the American trade union movement, consult Carroll R. Daugherty, *Labor Problems in American Industry* (Boston, 1933), chapters 10–12; Selig Perlman, *A History of Trade Unionism in the United States* (New York, 1922); Selig Perlman and Philip Taft, *History of Labor in the United States, 1896–1932* (New York, 1935); and Emanuel Stein and Jerome Davis, eds., *Labor Problems in America* (New York, 1940), chapters 13–20. Brief and somewhat popularized histories of American labor include Mary R. Beard, *A Short History of the American Labor Movement* (New York, 1920); Harold U. Faulkner and Tyler Kepner, *America, Its History and People* (New York, 1934); and Aleine Austin, *The Labor Story* (New York, 1949).

The hearings of Congressional committees form perhaps the best available sources of material on the controversy over industry-wide bargaining. Introduced at these hearings are statements from business and labor leaders, from governmental officials, and from economists. The Taft-Hartley hearings in the Senate are catalogued as the *Hearings before the Committee on Labor and Public Welfare,* United States Senate, Eightieth Congress, First Session, on S. 55 and S. J. Res. 22, Parts I–IV. Among the more interesting witnesses to offer testimony on industry-wide bargaining at these hearings are the following: James D. Francis (p. 244); Secretary of Labor Lewis B. Schwellenbach (p. 78); Theodore Iserman (p. 159); Louis Waldman (p. 398); Harvey W. Brown (p. 1603); A. F. Whitney (p. 2113); Gerald D. Reilly (p. 2053); and David A. McCabe (p. 2251). Other testimony on the subject is to be found in the *Hearings of the Senate Committee on Education and Labor on the National Labor Relations Act, 1939,* Parts 1–16, and in the *Hearings before the Committee on Banking and Currency,* United States Senate, Eighty-first Congress, First Session, on "Economic Power of Labor Organizations," Parts I and II, 1949.

Two postwar studies of American labor policies are worthy of mention. Harold W. Metz and Meyer Jacobstein, *A National Labor Policy* (Brookings Institution, 1947), is a strong statement against industry-wide bargaining. The Report and Recommendations of the Labor Committee of the Twentieth Century Fund, chaired by William H. Davis, formerly chairman of the National War Labor Board, is published as chapter 15 in *Trends in Collective Bargaining* (cited above). This report recommends that "managements and unions together explore the advantages arising from a wider application of market-wide collective bargaining."[1]

A Conference on Industry-wide Collective Bargaining at the Wharton School of Finance and Commerce of the University of Pennsylvania was held on May 14, 1948. The *Proceedings* were published by the University of Pennsylvania Press in 1949 as a part of an Industry-wide Collective Bargaining series. Two pamphlets in this series which are of great interest are Otto Pollak, *Social Implications of Industry-wide Bargaining*, and Bert W. Levy, *Multi-Employer Bargaining and the Anti-Trust Laws*.

An extended theoretical discussion has developed over whether unions possess monopolistic power over wages. A vigorous argument is developed by Henry C. Simons, "Some Reflections on Syndicalism," *Journal of Political Economy,* LII, No. 1 (March, 1944), 1–25, in opposition not only to industry-wide unionism but also to all collective bargaining as constituting a device for consmer exploitation. Arthur M. Ross, "The Influence of Unionism upon Earnings," *Quarterly Journal of Economics,* LII (February, 1948), 263–286, and Charles E. Lindblom, "The Union as a Monopoly," *Quarterly Journal of Economics,* LII (November, 1948), 671–697, have continued the argument over the monopoly power of unions. Also useful is Charles Edward Lindblom, *Unions and Capitalism* (New Haven, 1949). In Clinton Golden and Harold J. Ruttenberg, *The Dynamics of Industrial Democracy* (New York, 1942),

[1] P. 232.

chapter 10, industry-wide bargaining is considered a requisite for the sharing of the benefits of technological advances with labor.

A number of specialized studies have been made of the effects of industry-wide bargaining upon particular industries. These include Clark Kerr, "Collective Bargaining on the Pacific Coast," *Monthly Labor Review* (April, 1947), 650–674; *Collective Bargaining in the West Coast Paper Industry* (Princeton University, Industrial Relations Section, Department of Economic and Social Institutions, 1941); David A. McCabe, *National Collective Bargaining in the Pottery Industry* (Baltimore, 1932); Twentieth Century Fund, *How Collective Bargaining Works* (New York, 1942); and many others.

A valuable bibliography, which contains notations on several specialized studies, in addition to the more general works, was published by the Labor Relations Council of the Wharton School of Finance and Commerce of the University of Pennsylvania. It is: Selma P. Kessler, comp., *Industry-wide Collective Bargaining: An Annotated Bibliography* (Philadelphia, 1948).

For the experience with industry-wide bargaining abroad, see P. H. Norgren, *The Swedish Collective Bargaining System* (Cambridge, Mass., 1941); U. S. Department of Labor, *Report of the President's Commission on Industrial Relations in Sweden* (1938); and U. S. Department of Labor, *Report of the President's Commission on Industrial Relations in Great Britain* (1938).